John Clare

JOHN CLARE

from the portrait of 1820 by WILLIAM HILTON *by courtesy
of the Trustees of The National Portrait Gallery*

John Clare

John Lucas

Northcote House
in association with
The British Council

WRITERS AND THEIR WORK
Series Editors:
ISOBEL ARMSTRONG AND BRYAN LOUGHREY

First published in 1994 by Northcote House Publishers Ltd, Plymbridge House, Estover Road, Plymouth PL6 7PZ, United Kingdom.
Tel: Plymouth (0752) 735251. Fax: (0752) 695699. Telex: 45635.

British Library Cataloguing-in-Publication Data
A catalogue record for this book is available from the British Library

ISBN 0 7463 0729 2

Typeset by Kestrel Data, Exeter
Printed and bound in the United Kingdom by BPCC Wheatons Ltd, Exeter

for Arnold Rattenbury

'And still the grass eternal springs
Where castles stood and grandeur died.'

Acknowledgements

I owe a debt of gratitude to friends and colleagues with whom, over the years, I have discussed Clare. They include David Fussell, Roger Hubank, Tom Paulin and the poet-friend to whom this book is dedicated. Thanks, too, to another poet-friend, Matt Simpson, for a helpful suggestion. My largest debt is to yet another friend, Allan Chatburn. Without his prompting the book might not have been written; and without his insights it would certainly have been the poorer. It goes without saying that whatever faults remain are my responsibility alone.

Special thanks are due to Daveena Daley, whose impeccable skills made possible the delivery of a clean typescript to my publishers.

Contents

Biographical Outline

1793	John Clare born at Helpston, Northamptonshire, to Parker and Ann Clare. A twin sister does not survive.
1797	Mary Joyce born.
1799	Martha (Patty) Turner born.
c.1800	First meets Mary Joyce.
1804	New landlord of Parker Clare's cottage turns it into tenaments and raises rent.
1806	Buys Thomson's *The Seasons*. Begins to write verse.
1809	Act of Parliament passed, for enclosing Helpston, together with the nearby parishes of Maxey with Deepingate, Northborough, Exton, and Glinton (where Mary Joyce's family lived) with Peakirk.
1814	Buys his first 'blank book' from the bookseller, J. B. Henson, of Market Deeping.
c.1815	Relationship with Mary Joyce ends.
1818	Henson prints 'Proposals for publishing by subscription a Collection of Original Trifles, on miscellaneous subjects, religious and moral, in Verse, by John Clare, of Helpstone'.
1819	Edward Drury, Stamford bookseller, takes an interest in Clare's poetry. It is shown to the London publisher, John Taylor.
1820	16 January. *Poems Descriptive of Rural Life and Scenery* published. Later that month the Cato Street Conspirators tried and sentenced. March. First visit to London. Meets literati and has his portrait painted by William Hilton. 16 March. Marries Martha Turner at Casterton Magna. 2 June. Anna Maria Clare born.
1821	January. Fourth edition of *Poems Descriptive*, much

affected by Radstock's interference.

March. Finishes *Sketches in the Life of John Clare Written by Himself.*

*c.*March/April. John Drakard, a radical Stamford bookseller, publisher and friend of Clare's, is badly beaten. The Clares' landlord threatens to cut down the elms standing behind their cottage.

May. Taylor becomes owner/editor of the *London Magazine.*

September *The Village Minstrel* published.

1822	13 June. Eliza Louisa Clare born.
1823	May. Second edition of *The Village Minstrel* published.
1824	5 January. Frederick Clare born.
1826	16 June. John Clare, son, born.
1827	April. *The Shepherd's Calendar* published.
1828	29 April. William Parker Clare born.
1830	24 July. Sophia Clare born.
	Autumn. Swing riots across southern and midland counties.
1830–1	Contributes to Drakard's radical newspaper, the *Stamford Champion.*
1832	Moves to Northborough.
	First Reform Act. Cobbett enters Parliament.
1833	4 January. Charles Clare born.
1835	July. *The Rural Muse* published.
	December. Death of Clare's mother.
1837	June. Removed to Dr Matthew Allen's private asylum at High Beach, Essex.
1838	Mary Joyce dies.
1841	Writes *Child Harold* and *Don Juan.*
	July. Escapes from High Beach and walks back to Northborough. Writes about his *Journey Out of Essex.*
1843	Frederick Clare dies.
1844	Anna Maria Clare dies.
1846	Parker Clare dies.
1852	Charles Clare dies.
1864	20 May. John Clare dies.
	25 May. Buried at Helpston.

A Note on the Texts

Until recently Clare's writings – prose as well as poetry – have suffered dreadfully at the hands of his editors. Clare himself recalled that as an aspiring writer he had been determined to master the intricacies of grammar, but 'finding a jumble of words classed under this name, and that name and this such-a-figure of speech and that another-hard-worded figure, I turned from further notice of it in instant disgust. For, as I knew I could talk to be understood, I thought by the same method my writing might be made out as easy and proper. So in the teeth of grammar I pursued my literary journey as warm as usual' (*Sketches in the Life of John Clare Written by Himself*). Clare may have skipped clear of the teeth of grammar, but he has been repeatedly brought down by editors who have re-shaped stanzas, cut lines, sections of poems and poems in their entirety, regularly weeded out the fresh, lovely dialect words with which his work is thickly sown, and generally conspired, as I have remarked elsewhere, to make a great poet invisible. Now, thanks to the labours of Eric Robinson and others, we are beginning to get the work that Clare actually wrote. In what follows I have quoted from modern editions whenever possible. This may at first cause consternation among readers new to Clare. But read him as he ought to be read – with the ear as much as if not more than with the eye – and his work presents no difficulty.

Prologue

John Clare's first volume of poems was published early in 1820. Soon afterwards he was invited to London. The favourable reception of *Poems Descriptive of Rural Life and Scenery* had made him famous enough for the fashionable literati to want to meet the poet billed by his publisher as the 'Northamptonshire peasant'. For Clare, who had never before journeyed farther from his home village of Helpston than Newark-on-Trent, a distance of twenty-five miles, the trip was an epic undertaking.

> I started in the old Stamford Coach but I felt very awkward in my dress My mind was full of expectations all the way about the wonders of the town which I had often heard my parents tell storys about by the winter fire when I turnd to reccolections of the past by seeing some people at my old occupations of ploughboy & ditching in the fields by the road-side while I was lolling in a coach the novelty created such strange feelings that I coud almost fancy that my identity as well as my occupations had changd that I was not the same John Clare but that some stranger soul had jumped into my skin

These words form part of a planned autobiography which Clare undertook, so he says, 'in severe illness'. It isn't at all clear what the illness was. In early adolescence he had shown symptoms of what we would call *petit mal* (the milder form of epilepsy) and these symptoms seem to have recurred at later periods, although it is difficult to distinguish between them and the bouts of severe depression from which Clare also suffered and which may have been brought on by if they didn't occasion some pretty heavy drinking. Then again, Clare periodically took the 'blue pills' which had been prescribed for him by doctors and which, since they contained mercury, must have been offered as cures for venereal disease. There is no evidence to suggest that Clare did suffer from any form of venereal infection, but both before and after his marriage he had good reason to fear it as a possibility. He liked women and he seems to have tumbled into bed with several who took his fancy. There are, then, a number of possible explanations for his 'severe illness'. But deep within Clare's consciousness was a feeling of insecurity; and while that may not have been particularly acute in 1820 it had certainly become so by the time he sat down to write a prose account of his life. This began in 1821 at the prompting of his publisher, John Taylor, and he called this first attempt *Sketches in the Life of John Clare*. But the passage I have quoted comes from the unfinished *Autobiography*, on which he worked 1824–5. This is important.

Clare's coach journey almost uncannily anticipates the one taken by Pip in *Great Expectations*. And as Dickens's protagonist expects his journey to be a kind of rite of passage, transforming him from the identity of 'common labouring boy' to that of gentleman, so Clare must have felt that his arrival in London would mean that he could shed his identity of village labourer and emerge as Poet. By 1824 all this was in doubt. There had been no repeat to the success of *Poems Descriptive of Rural Life and Scenery*. His second volume, published in 1821, was respectfully but not especially warmly received; and sales, though by no means disastrous, were nowhere near to those of *Poems Descriptive*. Besides, his publishers, Taylor and Hessey, had maddeningly interfered with his work, sometimes at the behest of Clare's patron and others who busied themselves on his behalf, sometimes on their own account. They altered the volume's title from his own preferred *Ways in a Village* to the altogether more literary, anodyne *The Village Minstrel* (a title which sent signals to readers that Clare's work could be assimilated to the convention of poetry about and by the 'inspired' or natural 'genius' which James Beattie had popularized in his two-part poem *The Minstrel*, 1770 and 1774). Taylor also took upon himself the decision to drop a number of important poems and to truncate others. He questioned and frequently replaced Clare's use of idiomatic and dialect words and phrases. And at the insistence of Lord Radstock he struck out Clare's angry denunciations of enclosure. Taylor had persuaded Radstock to become the poet's patron, and Radstock, a large landowner and zealous evangelical, wasn't prepared to put up with what he called 'radical slang'. Add to these setbacks the fact that Taylor was showing few signs of wanting to publish *The Shepherd's Calendar*, the long poem which he himself had proposed as a suitable subject for

Clare's gifts; then tip in that Clare for all his early success had seen very little money come his way, so that he was forced back into his 'old occupations' (agricultural work from which he was repeatedly dragged by inquisitive London visitors wanting to interview the 'peasant poet', as a result of which fellow workers began to view him as a 'shirker' and/or getting above himself). Put all these matters together and it isn't surprising that the idea of writing his autobiography should have come to Clare at a time of 'severe illness'.

Autobiography is an attempt to make sense of a life. In his study of nineteenth-century working-class autobiography, *Bread, Knowledge and Freedom*, David Vincent tells us that when in 1831 Robert Southey presented the uneducated poet, John Jones, to the public, 'he commissioned from his protégé, *Some Account of the Writer*, and this autobiography could be added to those written earlier in the century by two genuinely talented rural poets, James Hogg and John Clare'. In fact Clare, as I have noted, made two attempts to write an autobiography. The first, *Sketches in the Life of John Clare*, was finished in 1821, when he was still hopeful of success, still thinking he could lay claim to public recognition as Poet. As with so much of his work, the *Sketches* were never published in his lifetime. But they were intended for publication. They are 'public' in that Clare expected them to be read. The unfinished *Autobiography*, on the other hand, though much of its material inevitably overlaps with the *Sketches*, comes at a darker and altogether more difficult moment. It is written out of a deep sense of crisis. When Clare says of the journey to London that he felt 'my identity as well as my occupations had changed', he is not playing with words. At the heart of his crisis lay a possibly unanswerable question. Just who *was* John Clare?

According to the monument erected to him in Helpston in 1869, five years after his death, he was 'The Northamptonshire Peasant Poet'. This echoes the title page to his first volume of poems, where he is identified as 'A Northamptonshire Peasant', and in a poem written late in life Clare acknowledged himself 'A peasant in his daily cares'. Two points need to be made about this, however. First, 'peasant' is a collective term which, as Cobbett angrily remarked in 1830, 'is a *new* word given to the *country labourers* by the insulting boroughmongering and loanmongering tribes'. Cobbett is wrong to claim that the term is a new one, but he is certainly right to protest that it has been imposed from outside. This is important because it points to a real difficulty Clare had when he needed to give a

3

collective name to the people among whom he lived and worked. He can call them by their professions: ploughboy, thresher, shepherd, hedger, ditcher, and so on. These are the exact terms of 'occupation'. But for a more general term he has either to fall back on 'peasant' or the even worse 'clown'. Such terms enforce a kind of conspiracy of degradation; and it isn't surprising that Clare tried to separate himself from 'clowns', most especially in *The Parish*, a poem on which he was working at the same year as he wrote his autobiography.

As to the second point. 'A peasant in his daily cares' is the penultimate line of a poem which ends with Clare proudly, defiantly, identifying himself as 'The poet in his joy'. The fact that he writes in the third person undoubtedly suggests the difficulty he by then had in feeling at ease with this identity. Nevertheless, his use of definite article and his insistence on 'joy' as defining the poet require us to understand that Clare is here linking the poet's essential self to the capacity for an emotion which Wordsworth – from whom Clare most probably took the word – regarded as proof of the authenticity of the poet's calling. It was quite literally evidence of divine inspiration. Clare aligns himself with the grandeur of a claim which is also made by Blake, Coleridge and Shelley (its ultimate point of reference in English poetry is Milton); and although there is a terrible poignancy in the fact that the poem in question was written in Northampton General Asylum, where Clare was placed in 1841 and where he stayed until his death, we have to recognize that he always saw poetry, *his* poetry, as a creative force which, because it was uncontaminated, made him free. Dreadful things were done to that poetry: in a multitude of ways it was undoubtedly contaminated. But not the source from which it came.

In The 'Progress of Rhyme', a kind of poetic *credo*, Clare invokes the word 'joy' on no fewer than ten occasions. And when as a boy he bought and first read Thomson's *The Seasons*, he said that it 'made my heart twitter with joy'. For Clare the word 'twitter' applies not only to birdsong but also the sprightly or glancing effect of waterlight reflected on stone or brickwork: as in 'The Village Minstrel', where 'the sunbeam twitterd on the wall'; and in *The Shepherd's Calendar* it is an effect of firelight: 'And warming pan reflecting bright/The crackling blazes twittering light' – 'January: A Cottage Evening'. Both aurally and visually the word invokes a relished shimmer of warmth, a glad lightness of being. It is the expressed source of poetry.

1

Beginnings

Clare's purchase of Thomson's *The Seasons* in 1806 marks his entry into print culture. It is a kind of rite of passage away from the oral culture into which he was born in Helpston, a small village in Northamptonshire not far from the borders of Lincolnshire and Cambridgeshire. His parents, Ann and Parker Clare, 'illiterate to the last degree' according to Clare, were agricultural labourers, although Ann's father, John Stimson, who was town shepherd to Castor, a town three miles away from Helpston, apparently thought Parker Clare beneath his daughter's notice. Perhaps because of this Ann was keen to get her son whatever education she could arrange for him. From an early age Clare found delight in reading. He also learnt to write, and although he never mastered orthodox spelling or punctuation, the fact that someone of his class could write at all was unusual at a time when such an accomplishment was discouraged by those who felt that reading was one thing – the poor ought to 'con' their Bibles and be able to understand notices – but that writing was quite another. (They might start framing petitions.) Parker Clare could read a little but he certainly couldn't write. On the other hand, he knew over a hundred ballads by heart, and he would often sing them to his family. Commentators tend to marvel at this and at his son's capacious memory for song, ballad and the Bible. But there is nothing unusual about this among people who have to depend upon memory; it's what oral culture is.

Clare drew on this culture and its traditions all his life. He loved the ballads he learned from his father and into which, as he sang them back, he would sometimes introduce verses of his own. (He also learned to pass off as the work of others his first attempts at poetry, which he'd recite to his parents in order to test their reaction.) This was common practice among 'uneducated' poets. In his essay on 'The Decline of Oral Tradition in Popular Culture', David Vincent remarks that 'we find the future [working-class poet] beginning his career as the composer of impromptu verses for neighbours, work-mates or lovers', and he quotes as examples the Cornish tin-miner John Harris, the Kettering weaver, J. A. Leatherland, and the customary weaver, Willy Thorn, all of whom left autobiographies in which they recount how they came into print culture via the oral tradition.

In such a tradition tunes may be important. They certainly mattered hugely to Clare. When in 1825 he wrote to his publisher, Taylor, to give him the correct name of the ballad 'Peggy Band', he told him that its tune is 'Capital as my father used to sing it but I cannot say much for the words for you know that the best of our old English ballads thats preserved by the memorys of our rustics (whatever they might have been) are so mutilated that they scarcly rise to mediocrity while their melodys are beautiful and the more I hear them the more I wish I'd skill enough in music to prick them down'.

Clare was in fact to teach himself skills enough to be able to transcribe the tunes of well over 200 ballads. He wrote out versions of such ballads as 'The Banks of Ivory', 'The Maid of Ocram: or Lord Gregory', and 'A Fine Old Ballad' ('Fare you well my own true love/And fare you well for a while'). He also taught himself to play the violin and would 'scrat' out these and other melodies. In a projected 'Essay on Popularity' he noted that 'paltry balladmongers' provide 'common minds' with something as 'old as England', that is, songs that 'still live on as common in every memory as the rain & Spring flowers'. And in 'The Village Minstrel' he remarks of his protagonist, Lubin, that

> as the load joggd hom ward down the lane
> When welcome night shut out the toiling day
> His followings markt the simple hearted swain
> Joying to listen on his homward way
> As rests warm rapture rousd the rustics lay
> And thread bare ballad from each quavering tongue
> As 'peggy bond' [sic] or the 'sweet month of may'
> As how he joyd to hear each 'good old song'
> That on nights pausing ear did echo loud and strong

Clare's deep commitment to this ballad tradition is crucial for a proper understanding of his work. When he said in 'The Progress of Rhyme' that 'I felt that I'd a right to song/And sung' he meant just that. Song is the condition from which much of his poetry comes and to which it returns. You can hear it in his verse patterns and rhymes, because for Clare rhyme is nearly always a 'marker', a way of signifying a line ending rather than offering the chance of exploiting the possibilities of reversal or surprise – or any of those many devices that belong to rhyme in print culture. And you can also sense the presence of song in his syntax. Clare makes the line the natural syntactical unit, as it commonly is in the song tradition. When Margaret Laidlaw, the mother of James Hogg, 'The Ettrick Shepherd', met Sir Walter Scott, she rebuked him for daring to enclose within a book – his famous collection of Border Minstrelsy – her favourite songs. 'There was never ane o my sangs prentit till ye prentit them yoursel, and ye hae spoilt them awthegether. They were made for singing an no for readin: by ye hae broken the charm noo, and they'll never be sung mair.' It isn't difficult to imagine Clare sympathizing with those words.

But as 'The Village Minstrel' also and contradictorily implies, Clare is all too aware that he's working within a print culture which for the most part unhesitatingly assumes that balladmongers are indeed 'paltry' and that village poets are no better than Lubins. And so he calls his minstrel by a name which links him with country 'clowns' (who are also present in 'the simple hearted swain' and 'rustics lay'). In other words, Clare recognized that the people he's writing for are a long way removed from – and feel themselves in every way superior to – those he is writing about. Like Dickens's Pip, Clare found himself moving into a culture where 'common minds' were at best to be condescended to and, more often, despised. The result is that on occasions he will align himself with those who condescend. He wants to show that he is above the society in which he grew. Hence, 'Lubin', 'clown', 'swain'. And there is no doubt that the journey to London and into print culture did lead him to feel in some ways separated from as well as irritated by the limitations of Helpston life. But at the same time he knew – if not at first then not long after his first visit to the metropolis – that he wouldn't ever be able to join the culture that beckoned so enticingly to him. And he also knew that the culture from which he came and which he was invited to despise had laid deep hold on him and was not to be disowned. And so, when he says that he felt he had 'a right to song', the word 'right' has about it a defiant pride, a resonance which is social and political. Clare was claiming a right that was everywhere being denied. What right, or rights, did the illiterate have?

The question isn't merely directed at the inadvisability of teaching the lower orders to write. Or rather, that issue is bound up in larger ones. In 'The Mores', a poem that was written between 1821 and 1824, Clare remarks bitterly that 'Inclosure came and trampled on the grave/Of labours rights and left the poor a slave'. The single most traumatic event in Clare's life was without doubt the enclosing of Helpston. By then he had already discovered how natural rights could be trampled on. During boyhood and adolescence he had been close to and probably in love with Mary Joyce, four years his junior and the daughter of a prosperous farmer in the neighbouring village of Glinton. The relationship was broken off in 1815-16, seemingly at her father's insistence. (Shades of Maria Beadnell, of Estella, of Grace Melbury.) Then again, when the landlord of the cottage which Parker Clare rented at £2 a year died in 1804, the new landlord converted the cottage into no fewer than four tenements and raised the annual rent for each to £3. The garden in which Parker Clare had delighted and from which he'd sold golden russet apples that more or less paid the rent was also divided up, and although Parker Clare retained the tiny plot where the apple tree grew, the family was now squeezed for both space and money. But bad though these things were, nothing affected Clare so adversely, deeply and permanently as the act of Parliament, passed in 1809, by which Helpston became an enclosed place. His world was literally changed out of recognition.

Enclosure was an evil for Clare, and thousands like him, not merely because of what it did, but because of what it represented: the power to destroy, to take away the dignity of the lives of the 'common minds' (and of course it's at this period that the word 'common' shifts from a descriptive to an evaluative range of meanings, all of them derogatory). It has been argued, by John Barrell among others, that the enclosure of Helpston by no means destroyed employment for agricultural labourers. Nor did it. But as Merryn and Raymond Williams have remarked, 'enclosure is the cry of [Clare's] class and generation against their fundamental subordination, concentrated in an outcry against the most immediate and most visible phase of change'. From now on Clare, in common with his

8

fellow labourers, was not free to wander across the land which he knew intimately and to which he felt himself to belong; and this taking away of knowledge, of relationship, as well as the despoilation of the land, operates as a determining factor in that prolonged crisis of identity which he underwent. On the one hand he was rooted in a culture which was quite literally being uprooted. On the other, he aspired to join a culture which was that of the uprooters.

Clare didn't much like the hard work of agricultural labour, and in his father's worsening rheumatism he had before him evidence of what the consequences of such labour could be. Parker Clare would eventually be reduced to breaking stones in order to earn a parish pittance. During his adolescence Clare went through a variety of jobs – potboy, gardener, lime-burner – and he even thought of joining the militia. He was by no means the first 'uneducated poet' to dream of escaping from hardship by earning a living as a writer. I have already noted that from an early age Clare's love of song led him to make up his own. His appetite for reading and, especially, poetry, led him to begin writing verse (he would often hide the results, which had been scribbled down on bits of paper filched from his mother, in gaps in the cottage walls). Then, in 1814, he began preserving his poems in 'a stoutly-bound volume of blank pages with a special title page', which he bought from the bookseller, J. B. Henson, at Market Deeping. Three years later Henson had become sufficiently impressed by Clare's work to suggest it should be published. Nothing came of the plan, because Clare couldn't find subscribers to finance the projected volume, but by now he was convinced that he had a future as a poet. So were others, notably the bookseller, Edward Drury, who had arrived in Stamford in 1817, and who took over the task of getting Clare's poems into print. This meant sending the poems out to publishers, and among those who received them, early in 1819, was Drury's London-based cousin, John Taylor. Taylor was already publishing work by, among others, William Hazlitt, Charles Lamb, De Quincey and Keats. The story of what happened next, and of Drury's dubious part in it, is too long to tell here (it has been well set out by the Tibbles and Edward Storey), but the upshot was that Taylor agreed to become Clare's publisher.

Clare was, not surprisingly, thrilled. He would be a writer. This was the quickest way out of a life of agricultural hardship. As he said in a letter, he was determined that he should never have to return to 'the Necessity of taking to hard Labour again'. No wonder then that after his initial break-through he should try his hand at various forms of writing. Quite apart from the *Sketches in the Life* (a very early example of what would become a norm later in the century among writers of his class), he began at least three novels – 'The Two Soldiers', 'The Stage-Coach', and 'The Parish Register'; he also started an essay-novel, 'The Bone and Cleaver Club', and a number of critical essays; and there were letters in 'Natural History', following the convention established by Gilbert White.

None of this work was published during his lifetime. Nor was the majority of his vast output of poems. Yet when *Poems Descriptive* came out in 1820 Clare must have imagined that he was at the beginning of a successful literary career. Good reviews, outstanding sales, lionization. There was however a problem. Clare was being marketed – the term is not too strong – in a manner that was intended to fit him into the tradition of 'peasant poets'. Eighteenth-century taste had included a taste for the primitive, and tastes exist in order to be satisfied. The most successful 'primitives' of the eighteenth century were Stephen Duck, the 'Thresher Poet', and Robert Burns. When Burns published what became known as the Kilmarnock edition of his poems, in 1786, he provided a tongue-in-cheek Preface in which he claimed that:

> The following trifles are not the production of the Poet who, with all the advantages of learned art, and perhaps amid the elegances and idlenesses of upper life, looks down for a rural theme, with an eye to Theocritus or Virgil . . . Unacquainted with the necessary requisites for commencing Poet by rule, he sings the sentiments and manners, he felt and saw in himself and his rustic compeers around him, in his and their native language.

Burns's claims for his ignorance of 'rule' are greatly exaggerated, but they were made, as he freely admitted to a friend, in order to help the sales of his poems. And they succeeded. Burns became the inspired natural genius *par excellence*. He was Beattie's Minstrel made flesh.

But Clare was different. Far less well educated than Burns, he nevertheless wanted to pass muster among those who represented 'upper life'. From boyhood onwards he read and read; even by the standards of his class he had a prodigious memory, and because he was an excellent mimic and had endless facility at making verses, he was able in his first volume to use, among much else, the trimeters that Dyer had chosen for the best-known version of his 'Grongar Hill' (1739), the Spenserian stanza-form of Shenstone's 'The Schoolmistress' (1737) and Beattie's 'The Minstrel', and the decasyllabic couplets of Goldsmith's 'Deserted Village' (1770). These are all poems which look down for a rural theme, and although to imply condescension in every case – Goldsmith's especially – would be unfair, they are certainly self-consciously 'literary' works. Add that *Poems Descriptive* includes a number of poems which are plainly within the 'picturesque' tradition of the pleasingly melancholic landscape, and you have a volume which aspires to a world of polite culture. So Clare, in the volume's key poem 'Helpstone', speaks of how he wishes for 'a better life' – one which the success of *Poems Descriptive* looked to have put within his reach, momentarily at least.

Taylor, however, wasn't at all keen to market Clare in those terms. His longish introduction to the volume begins:

> The following Poems will probably attract some notice by their intrinsic merit; but they are also entitled to attention from the circumstances under which they were written. They are the genuine productions of a young day-labourer in husbandry, who has had no advantages of education beyond others of his class; and though Poets in this country have seldom been fortunate men, yet he is, perhaps, the least favoured by circumstances, and the most destitute of friends, of any that ever existed.

Quite what Clare thought about this we don't know, but he can hardly have been overjoyed to find that his poems *as poems* would only 'probably' merit attention, and that to all intents and purposes he was so uneducated as to be illiterate. We do know, however, what he thought of Taylor's editorial interferences. And these need to be discussed in some detail because they set the pattern for Clare's writing life.

2

'All Beset'

'I am cursed mad about it', Clare wrote to Taylor's partner, Hessey, when he saw the third edition of *Poems Descriptive*. 'The judgement of T. is a button-hole lower in my opinion – it is good – but too subject to be tainted by medlars *false delicacy* damn it I hate it beyond everything.' Clare's anger is understandable. Yet again, Taylor had made cuts in the volume. He had decided to drop 'My Mary', Clare's affectionate but tough-minded parody of a well-known poem which William Cowper had written about his close friend, Mrs Mary Unwin, who had seen Cowper through recurrent bouts of acute depression and who was now becoming old and frail.

> Thy silver locks, once auburn bright,
> Are still more lovely in my sight
> Than golden beams of orient light

('My Mary')

That is Cowper, using a kind of scaled-down sapphic stanza. And this is Clare.

> Who low in stature thick and fat
> Turns brown from going without a hat?
> Though not a pin the worse for that

('My Mary')

'My Mary' joined 'The Ways of the Wake' or 'Dolly's Mistake', which had been dropped from the second edition of *Poems Descriptive*. George Deacon, in *John Clare and the Folk Tradition*, has shown that Clare's poem is adapted from a well-known broadside ballad, 'The Milkmaid Got with Child at the Wake'. In Clare's version the girl tells of her ruin by her faithless lover, Ralph, who is

> always a talking 'bout wedding expenses
> And the ages he's gotten to take;
> Too plain I can see through his evil pretences
> Too late I found out the mistake.

There is no reason to think that left to himself Taylor would have greatly objected to either poem, even though 'My Mary' suggested that Clare was rather better read than a peasant poet of pure inspiration was supposed to be. Taylor had certainly exercised editorial rights over the first edition, but these were mostly in the interests of making the poems conform to standard spelling, punctuation and lay-out of stanzas, although he had also taken it upon himself to drop a number of local or idiomatic words for which Clare hadn't thanked him. But this was different. This was censorship, and it was being carried out at the bidding of the man Taylor had found to act as Clare's patron, Lord Radstock.

A less suitable patron would be difficult to imagine. Radstock was of course a man of wealth. A profitable career at sea had helped him become a large landowner. Perhaps Taylor thought that this, together with the fact that Radstock was author of a book called *The Cottager's Friend* (1816) and his familiarity with many people of importance, made him a good choice to promote Clare's interests. If so, he should have thought again. For as Radstock's book made plain, he was an evangelical; he believed that the poor should know their place and thank God for it. (The cottager's friend was the Bible which, Radstock told his intended readers, was there to provide spiritual sustenance whenever the pinch of hunger or poverty was getting too keen.) In the period between 1800 and 1820 evangelicalism was a most powerful intrusive force in people's lives. Evangelicals were for Sunday observance, against infidelity, for censorship, against alcohol. And since they included leading churchmen, bankers and politicians among their number, they usually got their way. They were also philanthropists (but as Blake had said, 'Pity would be no more./If we did not make somebody poor'). Radstock served on no fewer than eighteen charitable societies; he was also a member of the Society for the Suppression of Vice which in 1817 had declared its aims to be the suppression of (1) Sabbath-breaking; (2) blasphemous and licentious books, prints, drawings, toys and snuff-boxes; and (3) private theatricals, fairs, brothels, dram-shops, gaming-houses, illegal lotteries and fortune-tellers. Among its successes was the 1822 prosecution of a bookseller for selling Shelley's *Queen Mab*, 'a publication of infidel character'.

Aware of which side his bread was buttered, Clare occasionally managed to make some kind noises about Radstock, but his real feelings come out in his explosion to Hessey about 'medlars *false delicacy*'. He must also have let slip his feelings to Mrs Emmerson, a London lady who had taken Clare up, because she told him that 'Your extraordinary patronage, will I hope remove from your mind those prejudices against the Great! – which your humble station made you *too keenly* feel'. Admittedly this was written in February 1820, before the worst had happened, but Taylor's readiness to bow the knee to Radstock would have confirmed Clare in his 'prejudices'.

To make matters worse, it wasn't just Radstock's 'false delicacy' that led him to demand cuts. False delicacy would explain why 'My Mary' and 'The Ways of the Wake' had to go. But there was also Clare's 'radical slang'. And so, for the fourth edition of *Poems Descriptive*, Radstock demanded that further cuts be made. Some lines in the key poem 'Helpstone', which Radstock found were especially offensive, were to be removed. To be fair to Taylor, he did protest, but in the end he gave way. 'Damn that canting way of being forced to please', Clare exploded to his publisher. 'I cant abide it and one day or other I will show my Independence more strongly than ever'. His rage is understandable – as understandable as Radstock's objection to the following lines.

> Oh who could see my dear green willows fall
> What feeling heart but dropped a tear for all
> Accursed wealth o'er bounding human laws
> Of every evil thou remainst the cause
> Victims of want those wretches such as me
> Too truly lay their wretchedness to thee
> Thou art the bar that keeps from being fed
> And thine our loss of labour and of bread
> Thou art the cause that levels every tree
> And woods bow down to clear a way for thee

This attack on enclosure is certainly radical. It even seeks religious sanction in calling wealth gained by enclosure 'accursed' and a cause of evil. Its Miltonic echoes are important because they show that Clare took Milton as unquestionably the great radical voice of English poetry. In his *Autobiography* Clare said that 'I read Thomson's *Seasons* and Milton's *Paradise Lost* thro when I was a boy & they are the only books of poetry that I have regularly read through'. When he speaks of wealth 'o'er bounding human laws', he has in mind Milton's Satan who, seeking illegally to enter Eden, 'Due entrance . . . disdained, and in contempt/At one slight bound high overleaped all bound' (*Paradise Lost* Book IV). This is not at all what an evangelical landowner expects of a poet he's chosen to patronize.

Given this, we may wonder why Radstock didn't demand that 'Impromptu: On Winter' be omitted from *Poems Descriptive*. Here, Clare speaks of 'Paltry proudlings hard to thee,/Dead to all humanity'. But the point is that such lines imply the need for charity, and Radstock had nothing against that, as long as those seeking it were properly humble. He would therefore have regarded 'Impromptu: On Winter' as quite acceptable. And the same can be said for another early poem, the 'Address to Plenty', which Clare dates as having been written in 1816, and in which he implores the rich: 'Freely let your bounty flow/On the sons of want and woe'. But 'Helpstone' is a very different matter. Clare makes the woods humbly 'bow down to clear a way for thee', and in that wonderfully vicious pun he plays on the cutting down of the trees as also implying that, like the helpless poor, they conspire in their own degradation: bow in fawning servility. Such deference! Radstock was right to sense the radical intent within these lines, one that recurs again and again in Clare's writing. He understood, as Clare's commentators have not, that Clare is drawing on a language which was the common property of radical politics in the early years of the nineteenth century. This requires some explanation.

There are two major concerns of radical politics at this period. One is the rights of labour. Thomas Paine's *Rights of Man* (1792) had provided a language which made possible the proclamation of 'labours rights'. (As we have seen, Clare uses this phrase in 'The Mores'.) The other concern is best expressed through the militant radicalism of Thomas Spence who, from the 1790s onwards, had been insisting that the land should be owned by the people. Put these two together and you get the radical debates and, more important, activities which are a powerful feature of the period 1800–20. So, for example, the Spa Fields Rising of 1816 was prompted by its organizers' insistence that 'The Practical Establishment of Spence's Plan [would] be an effectual remedy for the present distresses'. At the trial for High Treason of one of its instigators, a piece of paper, said to have been found in his pocket, was read to the court. 'Query: Have all men a right to equal participation in land? A. Yes.' A year later, when the men of Pentrich in Derbyshire went on trial for their abortive rising, a prosecution witness claimed to have been handed a piece of paper by one of the accused, Thomas Bacon, which said the 'property should be equalised and there would be eight acres of land for each individual'. (Bacon was also accused of complaining that he couldn't expect a fair trial because 'the prisoners are not tried by their Peers but by men of property'.) During the trial of the Cato Street Conspirators, surprised and arrested on 22 February 1820 as they were about to try to put into operation their plan to assassinate the entire cabinet, evidence was given that their watchword was 'resistance to oppression is obedience to our god', and that the oppressors were those who took land away from the poor.

This language and the convictions which it expresses were the common currency of radical egalitarianism. In early 1819, before the infamous Peterloo Massacre, the Spencean poet E. J. Blandford published several poems in the radical newspaper *Medusa* (motto: 'Let's Die like Men, and not be Sold as Slaves'). Among his verses is the following.

> Thus all the world BELONGS to Man
> But NOT to kings and lords;
> A country's land's the people's farm,
> And all that it affords:
> For why? divide it how you will,
> 'Tis all the people's still:
> The people's county, parish, town,
> They build, defend and till.

Verses like these were recited or sung in the many 'free and easies' set up in public houses in London during these years. Small wonder the Society for the Suppression of Vice was against such places.

(For much of the information contained in the foregoing paragraphs I am indebted to David Worrall's book, *Radical Culture: Discourse, Resistance and Surveillance, 1790–1820*.)

In a letter to Taylor dated 19 April 1820, Clare enclosed a poem called 'England', which took for its epigraph Cowper's famous 'England with all thy faults I love thee still'. The poem denounces 'pretenders' who 'arise for thy freedom/Alas but false prophets the best of 'em be'. 'England be patient', Clare implores: 'Still better slaves in a land of our own,/Then yield up to traitors in vainess aspiring/& banishd as slaves into deserts unknown.' At the time Clare wrote those lines the Cato Street Conspirators were awaiting execution. Others had been transported, 'banishd as slaves into deserts unknown'. Clare must here be referring to the conspirators, and that he should call them slaves makes clear his understanding of the desperate predicament of radicals who wanted to claim their rights but who in so doing risked greater slavery than they already endured. At his trial as one of the instigators of the Spa Fields Rising, James Wilson, Jnr. asked whether the king ought to be allowed to 'trample on [his people's] rights and privileges as Englishmen . . . Will Englishmen any longer suffer themselves to be trod upon like the Poor African slaves in the West Indies?'

Clare will draw on such language when in 'The Mores' he says that the enclosers 'came and trampled on the grave/Of labours rights and left the poor a slave'. But in April 1820 he must have felt the need to cover up. (It is possible but not, I think, likely that as a published poet Clare is wanting to identify with the 'England' of the poem: he wouldn't be the first or last working-class writer to yearn for acceptance by a culture which has appropriated Englishness.) And so, although in 'England' he says that 'Warm are my wishes that thou shouldst be free', he adds that such freedom will come, not now, but sometime in the future: 'Wait & there doubtless may heroes be born thee/Yet may the day come when thou shalt be free'. Perhaps he was worried that Taylor would think again about agreeing to publish further work by a poet who in 'Helpstone' had clearly identified himself with the radical cause and, by implication, with those who had been brought to trial: the men of Spa Fields, Pentrich and Cato Street. If so, who can blame him? He was living in dangerous times. Certainly his insistence that 'loss of labour and of bread' has been brought about by the enclosers as a satanic force 'stealing' into Eden should remind us – it would have reminded his first readers, Radstock included – that Milton calls Satan 'this first grand thief'.

Nor was it 'Helpstone' alone that Clare would have felt nervous about. In 1818 he had written a poem called 'The Lamentations of Round-Oak Waters', which uses the stanza form – common measure, but of eight rather than four lines – that Blandford also used in the lines quoted above (and which was no doubt a staple form of political ballad). 'Lamentations' combines pastoral elegy (for the early death of Clare's boyhood friend, Richard Turnhill) with a more general lament for the lost delights of a favourite spot of ground. The few commentators who have discussed the poem make reference to Clare's use of *prosopopaeia* (personification) both here and in 'The Lament of Swordy Well' (written 1821–4 but not published in his lifetime), and see in it – to quote one of them – a device to show that 'the rustic poet [finds] nature more humane than society'. Well, yes, but the device is common enough in folk song and ballad. What gives Clare's use of it its edge ought to be apparent from his title. 'Lamentations' looks back to the Old Testament he had read and whole passages of which he knew by heart.

Whether Clare recalled that in the Lamentations of Jeremiah the voice of the forlorn city of Jerusalem at one point complains that God 'hath inclosed my ways with hewn stone, he hath made my paths crooked' (3: 9) I don't know. Nor does it much matter. What does, is that in Clare's poem the water should itself speak and in so doing identify herself (for the voice seems to be gendered) with the kind of voice that Jeremiah gives to Jerusalem when she mourns that 'The Lord hath given me into [my enemies'] hands, from whom I am not able to rise up'. In Clare's poem this voice is as much a victim as the poet, who has in the poem's opening lines presented himself as helpless before those 'money'd men' who 'delight/More cutting then the storm/To make a sport and prove their might/O'er me a fellow worm'. 'Cutting' is no mere figure of speech. Certainly it plays on social contempt. The 1811 *Dictionary of the Vulgar Tongue* gives the meaning of 'cut' as 'To renounce acquaintance with anyone', and the most wounding 'cut' is the one that makes a person aware of his/her social inferiority. But 'cutting' in Clare's poem also directs us to those aggressive, even rapacious instruments of power, the plough and the axe, which between them hack through and strip the land, leaving it 'naked', bare of its trees and bushes. 'The greens and Meadows and the moors/Are all cut up and done', and as for the willows that 'flourished here/Hard as the axe that cut them down/ The senseless wretches were'. But the wretches (a term we have seen used in 'Helpstone') are themselves victims: 'sweating slaves,/Slaves by wealth decreed', because although they cut down the willows, 'Yet 'twas not them that own'd the field/Nor plan'd its overthrow'. As with the grovelling trees of 'Helpstone', these labourers conspire

in their own degradation: they 'cut' the land at the command of
those who 'cut' them.

The poem ends with the voice of the Waters offering a kind of
consolation: put up with your sufferings here, the rich will get their
deserts later.

> 'Ah cruel foes with plenty blest
>   So ankering after more
> To lay the greens and pastures waste
>   Which profitted before
> Poor greedy souls – what would they have
>   Beyond their plenty given?
> Will riches keep 'em from the grave?
>   Or buy their rest in heaven?'

In her discussion of 'Lamentations' in *John Clare: The Bounds of
Circumstance*, Johanne Clare compares the poem to Wordsworth's
'Michael'. She takes the superiority of 'Michael' for granted, but adds
that 'in spite of their obvious differences of quality and emphasis
"Michael" and "Round-Oak Waters" are founded upon a common
recognition: that the relationship between the rustic and his local
landscape had a precious shape and meaning which far trancended
the reason of necessity and utility'. I agree that Wordsworth's is the
greater poem, but it is also decidedly evasive about why Michael
loses his land. Or rather, Wordsworth *seems* to mourn for the general
loss of a way of life, of the hill farmers or 'statesmen' of Cumberland,
which in Michael's case then turns out to have a particular cause (he
unwisely allowed his land to be a bond of guarantee for a cousin
whose debt is called in). This hasn't much to do with necessity or
utility. Nor has it in Clare's poem. Necessity is the tyrant's plea.
Before enclosure, Clare says, the land 'proffited'. But of course it
profited those who worked it. Now, it is to profit others: those who
have enclosed it and who make others work on it, but not for
themselves. These wretches are the 'sweating slaves' who are made
to destroy a known, loved place. At the end of 'Michael' we are told
that 'the ploughshare has been through the ground/On which [the
cottage] stood' that was Michael's dwelling and abode; and the
impersonal form has the effect of implying that what happened was
inevitable, that nobody was responsible for it. This cancels human
agency. And yet someone must have become owner of the land and

put it under the plough. Clare's radical awareness means that he focuses on the agents of change: the 'greedy souls'. Wordsworth tries to evade the issue. That he should do so owes something to his growing conservatism. It also owes something to the fact that he, too, was becoming a landowner. As a result he chooses not to confront an issue of which 'Lamentations' rightly makes much: the cancelling of labour's rights by 'money'd men' who have turned justice into an instrument of class oppression. Those who have grabbed the land of Round-Oak Waters are

> lawless foes
> And l – s thems – s they hold
> Which clipt-wing'd Justice cant oppose
> But forced [and] yields to G – d
> These are the f – s of mine and me
> These all our R – ns plan'd
> Altho they never felld a tree
> Or took a tool in hand

The gaps in the text here are Clare's own and perhaps indicate a fear that what he'd said was dangerously close to being actionable, or that he wanted it so to be seen. At all events Taylor must have felt it prudent to leave 'Lamentations' out of *Poems Descriptive*. And, as with many of Clare's finest poems, it was never published in his lifetime.

In his biography of Clare, *The Right to Song*, Edward Storey remarks that with the enclosure of Helpston 'the whole of [Clare's] native landscape was to disappear under the plough. A landscape whose "only bondage was the circling sky" was being fenced and staked out for someone else's gain'. This is so, and the impact on Clare was absolute. His response could be one of bitter anger at those 'greedy souls' who had taken away labour's rights. But what lies beneath the anger is a deeper, more primal, outraged emotion. Johanne Clare's account of the relationship between rustic and landscape as having 'a precious shape and meaning' will not make sense unless we accept that the relationship is one of love, and of the intensest kind.

It is of course true that when Clare speaks in many of his descriptive poems of how he 'loves' to remark features of the landscape he is doing no more than echo the language of picturesque poetry. In such poetry the poet walks out, usually at evening, and catalogues a series of sights and sounds which between them 'compose' a verbal picture intended to produce soothing thoughts: of a 'pleasing melancholy' (for evening suggests the passing of things) and of nature's tranquil beauty (from which a benevolent deity can be inferred). The poetry of the picturesque is a way of aestheticizing landscape. In drawing attention to certain of its details, the poet by implication justifies his own good taste, his ability to harmonize a landscape of apparently disparate features. 'Love' in this sense is a matter of artistic judgement. And so, in 'An Evening Walk', Wordsworth says that 'I love to mark the quarry's moving trains,/Dwarf-panniered steeds, and men, and numerous wains'; and in 'Descriptive Sketches' he tells how 'By silent cottage-doors, the peasant's home,/Left vacant for the day, I love to roam' These are early poems, fully within the mode of the picturesque, especially in their ability to drain the scenes of real human meaning. Nobody actually works in these landscapes, or if they do their work is seen from afar and therefore made insignificant. Hence, the 'dwarf-panniered steeds' which Wordsworth can just make out in the distance. The founder of the picturesque, William Gilpin, had remarked that 'peasants engaged in their several professions' should be excluded from picturesque landscapes. 'Painting [is] a kind of poetry, which excludes all vulgarisms'. Given this, it should come as no surprise that Gilpin also wanted to exclude the vulgar.

But Clare *is* vulgar ('vulgar: common, customary, ordinary', *OED*). Not only is he one of the common people, but in his descriptive poems he refuses to remain within the bounds of good taste. He doesn't see things from afar. He doesn't stand on a prospect in order to survey the scene and look down on it, as was typical of picturesque poetry and painting (in a manner that had been established by the ideal landscapes of Claude Lorraine); nor does he walk round it. On the contrary, he walks *through* it. He wanders about it. Love for him goes with freedom to relate to a place that is intimately known and named, to which he *belongs*. Here, we should note that 'wandering' is a key term and concept of the period. It has to do with natural ownership of place and the right, therefore, not to be kept to allotted paths; and it also indicates moral, emotional and political freedom: the right to choose. And this is sanctioned by a mysterious but authentic transactional relationship that a person and/or community feels to exist between itself and place or chosen spot.

I wandered lonely as a cloud
That floats on high o'er vales and hills
When all at once I saw a crowd,
A host, of golden daffodils;
Beside the lake, beneath the trees,
Fluttering and dancing in the breeze.

The dancing daffodils become not merely the source of a deep, lasting joy; it is as though the very act of wandering has in some way led Wordsworth to them. Freedom has its own purposive intentions even though these can remain hidden or mysterious. 'When all at once': the phrase comes with the force of revelation. Moreover, the shift from 'crowd' to 'host' subtly implies a shift from nature indifferent to nature welcoming; for if 'host' means a large crowd it also means 'a person who receives or entertains guests'.

This is very close to something Clare said of the landscapes of de Wint, an artist of whom he was passionately fond and about whose art he wrote a sonnet. (De Wint would supply the frontispiece for *The Shepherd's Calendar*.) 'The sky & earth blends into a humanity of greetings' Clare remarked; and the words wonderfully catch the way in which in his poetry a known landscape is always a speaking/greeting one. Hence, for example, the moment in one of his very greatest poems, 'The Flitting', where he recalls walking in his native fields: 'And every weed and blossom too/Was looking upward in my face/With friendships welcome "how do ye do" '. Hence, too, Round-Oak Waters speaking to the poet, reminded him that there before enclosure 'Thou didst joy and love to sit/The briars and brakes among'. Such joy, such love, are born of relationship with the land. The forcible taking away of this land is, then, an act of rape and despoliation. It enforces a terrible degradation.

Dire nakedness oer all prevails
  Yon fallows bare and brown
Is all beset wi' posts and rails
  And turned upside down
The gentley curving darksome bawks
  That stript the Cornfields o'er
And prov'd the Shepherds daily walks
  Now prove his walks no more
And now along the elting land
  Poor swains are forc'd to maul . . .

You won't find any reference to baulks (a grassy ridge between two furrows) in poetry of the picturesque, any more than you will find a local, dialect word such as 'elting' (damp). Despite a bow in the direction of conventional pastoral in 'swains', and what that tells of Clare's hesitancy over his own position, the fact is that this land can be known, and only known, through a language so lovingly precise as to put it at the opposite extreme from the formulaic language of literary, pastoral poetry. In a letter of 1832 to his friend Thomas Pringle, Clare said that he was astonished when critics imagined that 'I had coined words which were as common around me as the grass under my feet'. No wonder he should say of Keats that 'his descriptions of scenery are often very fine but as it is the case with other inhabitants of great cities he often described nature as she appeared to his fancies & not as he would have described her had he witnessed the things he described'. And no wonder he should write scornfully of pastoral poems which

> are full of nothing but the old threadbare epithets of 'sweet singing cuckoo' 'love lorn nightingale' 'fond turtles' 'sparkling brooks' 'green meadows' 'leafy woods' etc these make up the creation of Pastoral and descriptive poetry and every thing else is reckond low and vulgar in fact they are to rustic for the fashionable or prevailing system of ryhme

That prevailing system was what his publishers always tried to force on him. Again and again they urged him to 'elevate' his subject matter, rather than dwell on familiar, common things. Clare was right to resent their stripping his poems of the 'low and vulgar' language in which he was steeped and which would, later in his life, make it possible for him to supply half of the words that make up Anne Elizabeth Baker's *Glossary of Northamptonshire Words and Phrases* (1854). And although there are moments when he does indeed seem to take an elevated view (as though he is adopting a stance appropriate to the making of a picturesque landscape), as for example in 'The Harvest Morning', where he writes of how 'labour sweats and toils and dreads the sultry day', the abstract word 'labour' operates in a manner different from Thomson, who is its source. In 'Summer', Thomson remarks 'even DRUDGERY himself,/As at the car he sweats, or dusty hews/The palace-stone, looks gay'. Thomson can write like this because he is projecting a view of a nation harmoniously combining to produce wealth for all. The exuberant vision of *The Seasons* (1730–48), with its confident sense of an unrivalled God-ordained fertility, of shared abundance, could hardly be sustained eighty years later, not anyway without requiring a view so elevated as to make invisible the fact that drudgery had turned into the wretchedness of near slavery. That was the labour which Clare had in mind. And where Wordsworth was always free to wander, Clare's people weren't. They were dispossessed of their once-native land; should they try to wander into it again they would be treated either as trespassers or poachers. For this is the period in English history when, as Corrigan and Sayer note in their book *The Great Arch: English State Formation as Cultural Revolution*, 'the most comprehensive battery of legislative, practical and other regulatory devices against the working-class is . . . established'. Hence, 'Lamentations' and the offensive lines of 'Helpstone'.

Hence, too, the conflict within John Clare. The Clare who journeyed to London in 1820 was a published poet, someone who could regard himself as having been invited into the world of cultural orthodoxy. He had become acceptable. Yet his deepest commitments were to those on the outside. These included not merely the immediate members of his family, but a wife. Two months after the publication of *Poems Descriptive* Clare married Martha (Patty) Turner at the church of Saints Peter and Paul, Great Casterton. By then Patty, whom Clare had first met in 1817, when she was 18, was seven months pregnant. Yet after the wedding bride and groom had to return separately to their parents' homes. They hadn't the money to set up house together and neither set of parents had room for the couple. Not until a month after the birth of their daughter, Anna Maria, on 2 June, was Clare able to 'fetch home Patty', and then only because the occupiers of the tenement next door to his parents moved out. Who then was John Clare? The success of *Poems Descriptive*, far from resolving the question, intensified it.

3

'The Poor Man's Delight'

Success brought him to the dinner tables of literary London. He sat there, looking in his grass-green coat and yellow waistcoat 'like a primrose', surrounded by, among others, Allan Cunningham, man of letters and editor, who would employ Clare as contributor to various of the journals he compiled, H. F. Cary, the translator of Dante, J. H. Reynolds, Keats's friend, William Hazlitt, the poet George Darley, and Charles Lamb. With these last two in particular he became friendly. Yet I suspect there was always a constrained quality about the friendships, and this seems borne out by Clare's letters to both men. The strain is also evident in increased signs of 'literariness' in poems he was now writing, some of which would find their way into his next collection.

Clare was impatient for the new volume to be published, Taylor less so. In 1921 the publisher was short of cash. He had bought the *London Magazine* for £500 and he was soon deeply involved in trying to obtain good contributors for the journal which, under the two-year editorship of John Scott, had gained a deserved reputation for the quality of its work. Taylor's decision to buy the *London* is understandable. It was an age when publishers began to take on their own, 'house', magazine. It was a way of 'puffing' their publications. Among the more obvious examples are *Blackwood's, MacMillan's, Bentley's Miscellany*. But Taylor lacked the kind of editing skills that had made the *London Magazine* a successful periodical, and it soon showed. He was under pressure. Then there were disagreements about Clare's use of dialect words and there must have been disagreements about the contents of the proposed volume. Most importantly, they couldn't agree about the title. Clare wanted *Ways in a Village*, but Taylor held out for *The Village Minstrel* and despite Clare's protests he had his way. Clare rightly complained that such a title would inevitably recall Beattie's *The Minstrel*, which had enjoyed something of a vogue since its publication (in two parts, 1770 and 1774), and which had been much imitated. *The Minstrel*, written in the Spensearian stanza which had become a staple verse form for literary pastoral in the eighteenth century, is a fairly drab rehearsal of the progress towards poetry of a natural genius, but at least it can be said that Beattie doesn't mean to condescend to his hero, Edwin. Edwin's genius 'proves' that poetic worth can arise anywhere and that 'natural', even 'barbaric', circumstance may favour it. *The Minstrel* presents the case for country over city, nature over nurture, as favourable to poetic genius. But *The Village Minstrel* is bound to hint at condescension. Apart from anything else, it points towards Clare himself as the minstrel in question. Yet in the longest poem in the volume, which bears the title 'The Village Minstrel', it is clear that Clare wanted to put some daylight between 'Lubin' and himself. Taylor's clumsy decision to make it the title poem, thus closing the gap, coupled with repeated delays over publication and a cluster of events which belong to the spring of 1821 and to which I shall refer later, go far to explain the depressions and anxieties which Clare experienced for much of the year. They may also help to explain his intermittent bouts of heavy drinking.

His mood wouldn't have been lightened by the reception of *The Village Minstrel*, which finally appeared, in two volumes, at the end of September 1821. Two thousand copies were printed but sales were sluggish, and while reviews were by no means all bad, they were for the most part more critical than the chorus of welcoming cries that had been made over *Poems Descriptive*. The *Monthly Review* must have hit especially hard. 'We do not conceive', the reviewer wrote, 'that occasional sweetness of expression or accurate delineation of mere exterior objects, can atone for a general deficiency of poetical language or the indulging in a style devoid of uniformity and consistency.' By 'poetical language' the reviewer no doubt meant all those stale epithets which Clare ridiculed in his attack on conventional pastoral poetry. The criticism of a style 'devoid of uniformity and consistency' is, however, altogether stronger. 'The Woodman', for example, is an uneasy anthology of effects. Clare's use of the Spenserian stanza and the poem's opening inevitably recall Keats's 'Eve of St Agnes': 'The beating snow clad bell wi' sounding dead/Hath clanked four' awkwardly introduces the much livelier account of how the woodman 'Dithers to view the rhymey feathered pane'. What follows is an odd mixture of exact observation of a winter scene ('The little birds sit chittering on the thorn', 'The squirking rabbit scarcly leaves her hole') and dull, even inept, generalizations: ('And nature all seemed sad and dying in despair'), swaddled in fustian ('Thanks to thy generous feeling gentle swain'). There is also a keyhole view of family prayers whose treacly piety would no doubt have gladdened Lord Rad- stock's heart.

> And ere he slept he always breathd a prayer
> 'I thank thee lord what thou to day didst give
> Sufficient strength to toil I bless thy care
> And thank thee still for what I may receive . . .
> Prepare thou me this wicked world to leave
> And fit my passage ere my race is run
> Tis all I beg o lord thy heavenly will be done' . . .

This out-evangelizes even Hannah More's assertion that the humility of the deserving poor was their best recommendation to heaven.

The Village Minstrel contains a number of other formulaic poems, among them 'Proposals for building a cottage' and 'Childish recollections', the former of which apes 'retirement' poetry (in which the poet announces that he plans to go gladly into solitude, the better to contemplate the deep meaning of life), while the latter tugs a forelock at the vogue for the kind of poem of which Thomas Hood's 'I remember', written a few years later, would act as market leader. There are also 'sonnets' – at all events they are poems of fourteen lines. 'I have been terribly plagued by the muses since I last saw you', Clare wrote to Taylor on 19 April 1820, 'I think I have wrote 50 sonnets'. Among those that found their way into *The Village Minstrel* is the following, called 'Summer'.

> How sweet when weary dropping on a bank
> Turning a look around on things that be
> Een feather headed grasses spindling rank
> A trembling to the breeze one loves to see
> And yellow buttercups where many a bee
> Comes buzzing to its head and bows it down
> And the great dragon fly wi gauzy wings
> In gilded coat of purple green or brown
> That on broad leaves of hazel basking clings
> Fond of the sunny day – and other things
> Past counting pleases one while thus I lye

> But still reflective pains are not forgot
> Summer sometimes shall bless this spot when I
> Hapt in the cold dark grave can heed it not

Say if you will that this isn't *really* a sonnet, that it obeys the rhyme scheme neither of the Elizabethan nor Petrarchan model and that the attempt to fill the fourteen lines leads to some desperate strategies (of which 'and other things' is the most blatant). The fact remains that the poem's interlaced rhymes allow Clare to move from detail to detail in a manner that he will learn to use to altogether greater effect in his marvellous bird poems, many of which are sonnets in the sense he understood and capitalized on: fourteen lines of rapid, intensely concentrated description. In 'Summer' he senses the need for the kind of ending that is often thought of as appropriate to sonnets; but although the final three lines compose a unit, it's one that, like the conclusion to a sonnet it recalls, Surrey's 'The soote season', can't really be said to have been prepared for; and Surrey at least detaches his closing couplet from what has gone before, whereas the rhyme of Clare's penultimate line is tangled up with a line with which it otherwise has nothing to do. 'Summer' is apprentice work right enough, but it prepares the way for those masterly Birds' Nest poems which are among the glories of our literature.

This brings me to 'The Village Minstrel' itself. Here, Clare tells the story of the discovery and growth of a poet who, among rural sights and sounds, 'fir'd with what he saw, humm'd o'er his simple song'. The poem, written almost inevitably in the Spenserian stanza, may seem to be a kind of apologia; and that was certainly how the *Monthly Review* saw it. 'The writer's mention of himself appears, in general, too egotistical and querulous.' Perhaps Clare anticipated some such criticism when he argued for calling the collection *Ways in a Village*. His proposed title keeps the emphasis on the social rather than the personal, let alone the egotistical. And yet in what turned out to be title poem Clare *doesn't* write about himself. This is how he introduces his protagonist.

> Young Lubin was a peasant from his birth:
> His sire a hind born to the flail and plough,
> To thump the corn out and to till the earth,
> The coarsest chance which nature's laws allow –

28

> To earn his living by a sweating brow:
> Thus Lubin's early days did rugged roll
> And mixt in timely toil – but e'en as now
> Ambitious prospects fir'd his little soul
> And fancy soared and sung, 'bove poverty's control.

In her detailed, sympathetic account of the poem, Johanne Clare suggests that at its end 'we take our leave of a character whose mind is filled not with plans and resolutions but with anxiety and doubt. And it is difficult not to believe that in Lubin's state of mind we may find some reflection of Clare's own longing and uncertainty in the early years of his career.' This is so, and it will help to explain why 'Lubin' rather than John Clare is the poem's protagonist, even though much of what happens to Lubin in the course of the poem had, as we know, happened to his creator. In wanting to open a gap between himself and his creation, Clare is surely trying to free himself from 'the coarsest chance which nature's laws allow', that is, snap the bonds that tie him to the image of 'peasant poet' which Taylor had by and large created. Taylor's insistence that the collection itself shouid be called *The Village Minstrel* is a way of enforcing this image.

Yet while Clare is not 'Lubin', the poem shows his deep commitment to the community in which he had grown up. Hence, the loving care with which he details how Lubin would listen to 'Some neighbouring labourer's superstitious tale,/How "Jinny-burnt-arse", with her wisp alight,/To drown a 'nighted traveller once did fail,/He knowing well the brook that whisper'd down the vale'. Taylor insisted on altering 'Jinny-burnt-arse', the local, labourer's term for marsh light, to the decorous 'Jack-a-lantern', but even so couldn't entirely damp the poem's joyous use of local lore, local language, the language of Clare's class. I have earlier quoted the lines in which Clare writes of the 'simple-hearted' swain's singing such ballads as 'Peggy Band' and 'Sweet Month of May'. Here he is noting Lubin's delight in country games.

> The 'fiery parrot' too, a laughing scene,
> Where two maids on a sheet invite the lout,
> Thrown o'er a water-tub to sit between
> And as he drops they rise, and let him swearing in.

In fact a major section of the poem provides a catalogue of ways in a village, which Clare draws a line under by saying that Lubin 'joined his mirth and fears with the low vulgar crew'. The poem wants to have it both ways. What is celebrated is also kept at a distance; condescended to as Clare loathed being condescended to. The 'literary poet' takes a stand far removed from 'the low vulgar crew', and scatters through his verses a language of 'literary' ruralism: swains, clowns, Hodge. But then the poem is also quick with the language of local custom, usage, reference. And this language can't be fobbed off on Lubin. It is *Clare's*. It is Clare, not Lubin, who talks of 'sliving nights', of a haunted place's 'squish-squash sound', of Lubin's 'searching for the pooty from the rushy dyke' ('pooty' = girdled snail shell), of the 'quawking of the swopping crows', of the bulrush's 'drowk head' ('drowk' = thirsty), and so on, and on. This is a poet absolutely unwilling to separate himself from the most truly exact and expressive language he knows, even though in the same poem, minding his literary manners, he will talk of 'Grey-girdled eve and morn of rosy hue', say that Lubin's rural muse 'warm'd his artless soul with feelings strong/To teach his reed to warble forth a song', refer to the 'jocund crew' that conducted the rural games, and so on, and on.

'The Village Minstrel' is in short a confused poem. Clare can't decide where he stands in relation to Lubin. His name suggests a put-down, but much of what Clare says about him and the community he comes from makes clear a commitment too complete to allow this planned condescension to survive. On the other hand, though Lubin yearns for the solitude that Clare also cherished, this isn't so much in order to separate himself from others as to preserve the interior freedom he needs if he is to make his poetry, whereas Clare does always seem to have been keen on keeping himself apart, and while this was temperamental it could lead to – and be seen by others as – a desire to preserve a distance between himself and his Helpston neighbours. We need then to note that the point at which the gap between Clare and his protagonist snaps shut is where he begins to write about enclosure, the subject which engages the last thirty of the poem's 120 stanzas.

> But who can tell the anguish of his mind,
> When reformation's formidable foes
> With civil war 'gainst nature's peace combin'd,

30

> And desolation struck her deadly blows,
> As curst improvement 'gan his fields inclose . . .

Who can tell? Why, John Clare, of course. And he proceeds to do so, in verse of gathering, angry eloquence. As with 'Round-Oak Waters', so here: 'nakedness' (the word recurs four times) becomes the cursed condition of a despoiled place; and the denial of freedom to wander is the mark of slavery.

> Inclosure came, and every path was stopt,
> Each tyrant fixt his sign where paths were found,
> To hint a traspass now who cross'd the ground:
> Justice is made to speak as they command;
> The high road now must be each stinted bound:
> – Inclosure, thou'rt a curse upon the land
> And tasteless was the wretch who thy existence plann'd

> O England! boasted land of liberty,
> With strangers still thou mayst thy title own,
> But thy poor slaves the alteration see,
> With many a loss to them the truth is known;
> Like emigrating birds thy freedom's flown,
> While mongrel clowns, low as their rooting plough,
> Disdain thy laws to put in force their own;
> And every village owns its tyrants now,
> And parish-slaves must live as parish-kings allow.

These lines, imperfect though they are, deserve our careful attention, not merely because of the way they focus an argument and direct its anger, but because in doing these things they make way for an accent very different from the one Johanne Clare finds in the poem's controlling voice. For her, that is characterized by its deference. 'The note of dissent', she says, 'is choked, cut off before it is fully articulated by the poet's argument.' Admittedly she has in mind here the poem's opening, where Clare says the 'humble rustic' finds 'toil and slavery bear each fancy down/. . . And force him to submit to fate's controlling will'. But by the end of the poem any pretence that the fate which controls 'toil and slavery' is inevitable – like the fate which consigns Gray's rustic genius to 'blush unseen' – or may not be thought of as caused by human agency, is knocked flat by the force of Clare's argument. And after all he is quite certain

31

that England's lost liberties go with a justice that has been bought by tyrants and 'village kings'. *This* is deference?

And yet, magnificently, scornfully eloquent though this part of the poem is, Clare knows that in speaking for Lubin he speaks for the defeated, for all those whose liberty has been lost. Hence, his sympathy for

> you, poor ragged outcasts of the land,
> That lug your shifting camps from green to green,
> He lov'd to see your humble dwellings stand,
> And thought your groups did beautify the scene

True, Clare goes on to say that the gipsies he here speaks to and for are 'to fate's hard want decreed', but 'fate' has to be read as shorthand for the activities and attitudes of those who regard gipsies as dangerous outlaws. And in an age where this was commonplace (as Jane Austen's *Emma* will remind us), Clare's championing of the 'ragged outcasts' must be read as an act of social and political defiance. The ragged are akin to the naked in being denied their dignity. Clare returns dignity to them, as far as poetry can, in verses in *The Village Minstrel* called 'The Gipsies Camp'.

Here, then, I need to note that Clare, who had from boyhood been fascinated by the 'gipsy tribe', will increasingly identify with outlaws and outcasts, whether these are human or hunted birds and animals. His imagination is drawn to those who are in every sense without the law, who exist on the margins, trying to assert freedom and liberty against the growing army of tyrants who have usurped those terms. In July 1821 he published a protest ballad in *Drakard's Stamford News* to which he gave the title 'The Rich and the Poor: Or Saint and Sinner'. (The poem was published anonymously and has been established only recently – by Eric Robinson – as Clare's. It can be found in Robinson's edition of *The Parish*.)

> The rich man has a cellar
> & a ready butler by him
> The poor man must steer
> For his pint of beer
> When the saint is sure to spy him . . .

> The rich man is invisible
> In the crowd of his gay society
> But the poor man's delight
> Is a sore in the sight
> & a stench in the nose of piety

John Drakard was a radical publisher, bookseller and newspaper editor who earlier in the year had, so Clare told Taylor, 'been severely beaten . . . in a rather cowardly way by a person coming with the excuse of buying a book . . . the stranger had a footman with him & is some one no doubt that the Paper has provokingly abused'. Whoever it was must have been a person of rank, one of the invisible rich 'in the crowd of his gay society'. 'Is Poor Scott gone' Clare asks in the same letter. John Scott, first editor of the *London Magazine*, had been injured in a duel with Jonathan Christie, a friend of Lockhart, editor of *Blackwood's*. According to J. C. Reid, the biographer of Thomas Hood, Scott was 'tempted into attack' on *Blackwood's*, the high tory magazine, because of Lockhart's 'vituperations'. Small good it did him. His injuries led to his death.

Clare must have felt that the ranks of tyrants were threatening to overwhelm him and his kind, especially since at more or less the same time the landlord of his parents' cottage announced that he was planning to cut down the two elms that had for many years stood over the cottage. On 7 March Clare wrote to Taylor, to say that he had heard of 'poor Scott's death' and then went on to tell him of this latest outrage.

> my two favourite Elm trees at the back of the hut are condemned to dye it shocks me to relate it but tis true the savage who owns them thinks they have done their best & now he wants to make use of the benefits he can get from selling them – O was this country Egypt & was I but a caliph the owner shoud loose his ears for his arragant presumption & the first wretch that buried his axe in their roots shoud hang on their branches as a terror to the rest

Taylor behaved well over this. He offered to buy the trees for Clare. Then the owner changed his mind and the trees were saved. But the threat to destroy them produced Clare's great poem, 'To A Fallen Elm'. In his introduction to *The Village Minstrel*, Taylor quotes Clare's letter and remarks perceptively that it shows the 'passionate regard of poor CLARE for things which were the landmarks of life, the depositories of almost all his joys'.

There is a precedent for Clare's poem. Taylor's acute remark about the elms being the depository 'of almost all his joys' could as well be applied to Robert Bloomfield's lovely poem, 'My Old Oak Table', which Clare, who was a passionate admirer of Bloomfield, certainly knew. It begins:

> Friend of my peaceful days, substantial friend,
> Whom wealth can never change, nor int'rest bend,
> I love thee like a child. Thou wert to me
> The dumb companion of my misery,
> And oft'ner of my joys; – then as I spoke,
> I shar'd thy sympathy, Old Heart of Oak!

The affectionate familiarity of this mode of speech is very close to the opening of Clare's poem, although Bloomfield's sustains its tender, intimate manner throughout, the table becoming associated with both domestic love and the poet's love of his art – he 'wrote "The Farmer's Boy" upon thy back!', whereas Clare's shifts from familiarity to attack the would-be wreckers of his domestic peace. This is how 'To A Fallen Elm' begins:

> Old elm that murmured in our chimney top
> The sweetest anthem autumn ever made
> And into mellow whispering calms would drop
> When showers fell on thy many coloured shade . . .
> How I did love to hear the winds upbraid
> Thy strength without while all within was mute
> It seasoned comfort to our hearts desire
> We felt thy kind protection like a friend

Friendship such as this is identified with, voiced through, the warmth of familiar speech – murmuring – and music, 'the sweetest anthem', which implies an almost sacred regard for all that is familiar, customary. But then the poem turns away from this language of loving regard to one of outrage. 'Self interest saw thee stand in freedom's ways/So thy old shadow must a tyrant be.' Self-interest and freedom are yoked together as evidence of contemporary cant: the wiggish *laisser-faire* which threatens custom and natural rights. Hence, the poem's great, whirring conclusion:

It grows the cant term of enslaving tools
To wrong another by the name of right
It grows a liscence with oer bearing fools
To cheat plain honesty by force of might
Thus came enclosure . . .
The rabbit had not where to make his den
And labours only cow was drove away
No matter – wrong was right and right was wrong
And freedoms bawl was sanction to the song

Such was thy ruin music making Elm
The rights of freedom was to injure thine
As thou wert served so would they overwhelm
In freedoms name the little that is mine
And these are knaves that brawl for better laws
And cant of tyranny in stronger powers
Who glut their vile unsatiated maws
And freedoms birthright from the weak devours

Clare brings together here the terms of popular radical protest we have seen him use on previous occasions, but now with altogether more force. The power of the lines is indeed so great as to seem almost out of proportion to the occasion, especially when we consider that in his letter to Taylor Clare had followed his outburst against 'the savage' by remarking that 'this mourning over trees is all foolishness . . . a second thought tells me I am a fool . . . this is my indisposition & you will laugh at it'. But the indisposition returned, prompted no doubt by his brooding over what had happened to Drakard and Scott, and by Taylor's delay over publishing the collection of poems that was stuck with that demeaning title, *The Village Minstrel*. Hence, the vibrant anger of 'To A Fallen Elm', a poem that was never to be published in Clare's lifetime, but whose rhetorical grandeur, the dramatic force of its public utterance – it begs to be spoken aloud – seems to me unequalled in English poetry, with the possible exception of Dryden. It recognizably works the same language of popular radicalism as the verses of E. J. Blandford and other, similar writers, but between them and Clare is all the difference that must exist between the work of competent versifiers and a great poet. As for Dryden, he could never have managed the considerate, loving tenderness of the poem's opening.

4

'A Labourer Sung'

Between 1821 and 1827 when *The Shepherd's Calendar* appeared, Clare published no new volume of poetry. But he wrote ceaselessly. Individual poems of his appeared in journals and magazines, often in such profusion that he decided to adopt the pseudonym of 'Percy Green'. They represent a mere fraction of the output of those years. Quite apart from the *Calendar* and another book-length poem, *The Parish*, of which more later, there were the *Sketches*, the *Autobiography*, there was a journal, there were essays and outlines for essays, there were shoals of letters; and, too, there were any number of poems – including poems about birds – of extraordinary quality. Nearly all this work was undertaken in circumstances that would have prevented most writers from ever putting pen to paper. Clare, Patty, and a growing family, continued to live in the part of the cottage they had moved into after the birth of their first child. It was now far too small for them, but lack of money meant that more suitable accommodation was out of the question. The steady erosion of his early reputation made Clare miserable, and ill-health added to money problems that were not lessened by Mrs Emmerson's insistence that, thanks to his patrons' generosity, Clare would be financially safe for the duration of his life. Some sort of trust fund had, it seems, been set up for him. But he saw precious little of it, and what he did receive was paid grudgingly and in arrears.

He did however continue to see something of the fashionable world. Or rather it chose to see him. Those anxious to observe the 'peasant poet' in his native habitat thought nothing of driving to Helpston to stare through the windows of his cottage; and when Clare was working in the fields they would summon him to come and talk to them. As I have already noted, his fellow workers took a dim view of this. Nor did he gain financially from such impertinence. His visitors seldom gave him anything other than a book (and not often that, for he had a sizeable collection and could therefore afford to buy his own, so they reasoned).

And at this difficult period his childhood sweetheart Mary Joyce re-entered his life. She had disappeared from view after her father had forbidden her to go on meeting him. Then, in the summer of 1821, he saw her for the first time in years. 'I have had the horrors agen upon me by once agen seeing devoted mary,' he wrote to Taylor on 11 August; and with the letter he enclosed some stanzas to which he gave the title 'Farewell to Mary'. 'Where is the heart thou once has won/Can cease to care about thee' the poem begins; the answer is, nowhere. In December of the same year he sent Taylor a poem called 'Hymn to Spring' – in which spring is personified in a manner that makes it remarkably like the woman to whom he'd announced his intention of bidding farewell.

> Thou virgin bliss the seasons bring
> Thou yet beloved in vain
> I long to hail thee gentle spring
> & meet thy face again

'Thou yet beloved in vain'. At some deep level Clare identified Mary Joyce with the spring of his life and so with the hopes of becoming a recognized poet. As a result she is made to stand for a compensatory dream of success and achieved love and in the later years of madness he will come to persuade himself that she is being kept from him.

Meanwhile, actualities pressed in. He was badly shaken by the death of Robert Bloomfield in 1823. The two poets had been planning to meet to discuss a biography that Clare hoped to write of the Suffolk poet. Clare deeply admired Bloomfield and in some respects thought of him as his master. Then came the news that Bloomfield was dead. Clare wrote three sonnets about him. Bloomfield's work, he says, 'is built on a more solid foundation' than fashion; and in the first of his sonnets he speaks with stark power of how it will survive when 'many a fame shall lie/A dead wreck on the shore of dark posterity'.

Then there was the continuing horror of enclosure. This is taken up in two key poems of the period, 'The Mores' and 'The Lament of Swordy Well'. They have been called poems or 'rural protest', although they are much more than that. In an invaluable essay, 'The

Time's Alteration: Popular Ballads, Rural Radicalism and William Cobbett', Alun Howkins and Ian C. Dyck note that a number of popular ballads belonging to the opening years of the nineteenth century share a 'conviction articulating a political solution to distress and a political diagnosis of its cause'. They quote one with which Clare was familiar, 'When This Old Hat Was New'. Its last two verses run:

> When Romans reigned in this land, the commons they did give,
> Unto the poor for charity, to help them for to live,
> But now they've taken the poor man's land, that certainly is true,
> Such cruelty did ne'er abound, when this old hat was new.

> Now the commons are taken in, and cottages are pulled down,
> And Molly has no wool to spin her linsey-woolsey gown;
> The winter cold, and clothing thin, and blankets very few,
> Such cruelty did ne'er abound, when this old hat was new.

You can naturally break these lines into the four- and three-stress lines of common measure which Clare had used for 'The Lamentations of Round-Oak Waters', and which he returns to in 'The Lament of Swordy Well'. He had also used this most habitual of all ballad forms in another anti-enclosure poem of *The Village Minstrel*, 'Helpstone Green', although that poem ended with a moralizing reflection which bowed to the 'principle of change' so beloved of the picturesque: 'As are the changes of the green/So is the life of man'. But in the 'Lament', as in the 'Lamentations', nature has its own voice.

> Im swordy well a piece of land
> Thats fell upon the town
> Who worked me till I couldnt stand
> And crush me now Im down

This voice speaks for all who have been forced 'onto the parish'. It could be the voice of Parker Clare who, after a lifetime of work in the fields and now crippled with rheumatism, was required to break stones for his pittance. The well's voice is unmistakably male. 'I am no man to whine or beg/But fond of freedom still', it asserts, and then:

> Yet worried with a greedy pack
> They rend and delve and tear
> The very grass from off my back
> Ive scarce a rag to wear . . .

'I feel so lorn in this disgrace', the well later laments, voicing that horror of 'nakedness' which we have seen deeply troubled, even appalled Clare, as it did all of his class. Howkins and Dyck point out that the extent of the labourer's new-found beggary was symbolized by his 'torn and tattered clothes', and to reinforce this point they quote a broadside version of the ballad 'The Roast Beef of Old England', which adapts the patriotic original of Henry Fielding in order to fit it to new, changed times: 'His garments, tho' homely, did comfort denote./He'd holyday linen, and holyday coat/ . . . Alas! what a change, and how altered the case!' They could just as well have quoted Clare's 'Lament'.

'The Mores' is different. It is written in couplets which combine great fluency with concentrated power; and it doesn't merely mourn the difference between past and present. Howkins and Dyck remark of 'My Old Hat' and ballads like it that in presenting this difference 'there is no clear sense of time – it is simply "former days" or "olden times" '. 'The Mores' however makes plain that change came when and because enclosure took the common land away from the common people. The poem begins with a recalled vision of the free land, of

> plains that stretched them far away
> In uncheckt shadows of green brown and grey
> Unbounded freedom ruled this wandering scene
> no fence of ownership crept in between . . .
> Now this sweet vision of my boyish hours
> Free as spring clouds and wild as summer flowers
> Is faded all – a hope that blossomed free
> And hath been once no more shall ever be

These lines are so dense with meaning that to unpack them all would take a book in itself. The 'uncheckt' shadows are not merely free to spread themselves, they don't conform to the 'tasteful' prescriptions of a picturesque landscape, including its 'chequered shades'. In other words, the moors are not 'composed', they are for real. In a lovely, witty oxymoron, freedom – the Englishmen's birthright – is made the only ruler of a scene over, through, and around which the eye can wander as it chooses: as, of course, can the free man. But now the 'sweet vision' of an Edenic land has been cancelled. Read these lines casually and it seems as though Clare is echoing the Wordsworth of 'Elegiac Stanzas' and the 'Immortality' ode. Read them more carefully and it becomes evident that he is challenging him. (Clare admired Wordsworth but he told Taylor that for all his great originality he also had great faults; and he had already parodied his 'nursery rhyme' style.) In Clare's poem, the vision has fled, not because shades of the prison-house begin to gather round the growing boy, but because that vision has been literally destroyed. 'A power has gone that nothing can restore,/A deep distress hath humanised my soul', Wordsworth had written in the 'Elegiac Stanzas'. He was mourning a brother lost at sea, victim of natural causes. But when Clare speaks of *his* faded vision which 'hath been once' but which 'no more shall ever be', he mourns for a land lost to him by the action of enclosers. This was *meant*. And so

> Fence now meets fence in owners little bounds
> Of field and meadow large as garden grounds
> In little parcels little minds to please . . .
> Each little tyrant with his little sign
> Shows where man claims earth glows no more divine
> On paths to freedom and to childhood dear
> A board sticks up to notice 'no road here'

There is an unsurpassable eloquence about the anger of these lines, their scornful denunciation of 'little tyrants'. You would certainly have to go back to Dryden to find any English poet capable of writing with such a confident public voice. And 'The Mores' is a public poem, a matter which isn't affected by its not having been published in Clare's lifetime. Its confident use of the language of popular radicalism is immeasurably helped by the hammering, rhetorical rhymes, which punch the argument home. And in his remark that the sign of prohibition 'Shows where man claims earth glows no more divine' we can hear a rebuke to the Wordsworthian claim that the visionary gleam of childhood will inevitably fade out. 'The things which I have seen I now can see no more', Wordsworth had written in the 'Immortality' ode. If Clare can't see them it is because the land has been so altered by tyrants as to make it unrecognizable.

'The Mores' was written some time between 1821 and 1824. In that latter year Clare gave serious thought to joining the Ranters, some of whose meetings he now attended. The 'Ranters' were primitive Methodists. They had broken away from the main body of Methodists earlier in the century because they saw that body as altogether too ready to sacrifice principles to expediency. The split is along class lines. Primitive Methodists were solidly working class. In choosing to align himself with them, and in telling his publishers of his intentions, Clare may have been trying to free himself from Radstock's endless concern for the state of his soul. His lordship regularly sent Clare what he considered to be suitably improving books and pamphlets. Edward Storey says that Radstock, who was 'constantly directing Clare's thoughts towards theology', pestered him to 'visit a clergyman for instruction'. On 20 April 1824, Clare informed Hessey that 'I have joined the Ranters . . . they are a set of simple sincere & communing christians with more zeal than knowledge earnest & happy in their devotions'. There is no reason to doubt the sincerity of his claim that 'in their company I can scarcly refrain from shedding tears', but it is important to note that the Ranters were involved in radical politics, like the seventeenth-century sect from whom their name was derived. The earlier Ranters were extreme communitarians. We know less about the politics of the later ones, but Ebenezer Elliott's poem 'The Ranter', published in 1834, helps fill in some gaps. Its hero, Miles Gordon, is a working-class man of Sheffield who for six days a week labours and on the seventh goes out into the countryside to preach. The poem is mostly taken up with the sermon which Gordon delivers to his working-class audience. He identifies himself with those preachers of the Commonwealth period who fought 'freedom's holy fight', and who taught the 'poor and broken-hearted' 'truths that tyrants dread and conscience loves'. Gordon prophesies that these tyrants will 'fall before thee – gone, their splendour'. The confidence of this may owe something to time and place: following the disappointments of the first Reform Act of 1832, working-class politics was entering a radical phase, and unionism was astir in the cities. But Gordon's language comes very close to the language we have seen Clare drawing on in his anti-enclosure poems. It is a language shared by otherwise distinct strands of popular radicalism, and its main concern is with the fact that the land has been taken away from the people.

Yet during the early 1820s Clare wavered between full

identification with that language, that politics, and keeping a distance from it. And we must surely recognize that his desire to be accepted by the world of his 'betters' had much to do with this. It will certainly explain the confusions of *The Parish*. In the introduction to his edition of this sprawling satiric poem – it runs to over 2,000 lines and is unfinished – Eric Robinson sets out the difficulties of dating it, although he is in no doubt that most of it was written between 1820 and 1824. These are the years of Clare's rise to fame and fall from it. Not surprisingly, perhaps, *The Parish*, while certainly a treasure-house of detail, is something of a muddle. Clare leans heavily on Goldsmith's strategy of shifting between past (good) and present (bad), and his balancing of precise accounts of individuals (which are for the most part remarkably well done) against general statements about village or parish life also owes a great deal to Goldsmith. But Clare's poem lacks a controlling point of view. What does he actually think of his parish? The short answer is that as a satirist he looks down on it, but that as he rather more frequently abandons satire for apologia the work can't help but be broken-backed. Not surprisingly, therefore, he continued to tinker with it. But it never satisfied him.

We can get a clue to his difficulties if we look at how he writes about a quack doctor.

> Thourt no great 'schollard' that the learned tell
> And all that buy thy drugs might know as well
> But it so turns and lucky for thy pelf
> Thy patients are less 'schollards' then thyself
> But what of learning words mispelt is small
> Drawbacks on knowledge that gives cures for all
>
> (11. 693–8)

The second paragraph rounds on the previous one, and rightly. Clare can't after all claim to be a 'schollard'. Yet *The Parish* often strikes the kind of satiric pose associated with Pope and his school: a tone of civilized learning is to provide the rapier thrust by means of which to dispatch the insufficiencies of the uncouth. Hence, Clare's comment on a farmer who sends to his local newspaper 'illspelt trash on patriotic cavils/Leaving correction to the printers devils' (11. 763–4) – as of course Clare himself was forced to do.

More interesting, perhaps, is the matter of Clare's patriotism. A section beginning at line 1,000 praises England as free 'From tyrant governments and broken laws/Since freedom came and crowned thee free none dare/As yet to raise thy lion from its lare'. This piece of flag-waving is close in spirit to a sonnet Clare enclosed in a letter to Taylor, dated 18 August 1821, ('England with pride I name thee'), and was probably written at about the same time. But this looks decidedly odd, coming as it does from the poet who had already written that scorching attack on England's fake liberties in 'The Village Minstrel', and who knew that, as he'd remarked in 'To A Fallen Elm', England was infested with those who 'Bawl freedom loud and then oppress the free'. Besides, much of his finest poetry voices awareness of lost freedoms. The patriotism of *The Parish* can be explained only if we assume that the poet-as-satirist is here presenting his credentials for joining polite society.

This will also explain why elsewhere in the poem Clare adopts the stance of 'the deferential worker', which Howard Newby, in his book of that title, sees as a 'combination of conservative deference and radical resentment'. I wouldn't myself think 'combination' the appropriate term to describe what is surely a contradiction, but at least Newby's term will help account for such forelock-tugging moments as the one where Clare grovellingly confesses that 'True Patriotism is a theme divine/And far above a theme so mean as mine' (11. 1036–7). How to square that note with the protest over the 'poor sinning starving clown' who meets 'jail and hanging for a stolen crown/While wealthy thieves with knaverys bribes endued/ Plunder their millions and are not pursued' (11. 1324–7).' What, in England! Surely not.

The Parish comes into its own where Clare more or less abandons satire. Here, the section on 'The Vicar' deserves to be singled out. In a letter to Taylor of May 1821, Clare describes this study, which he originally intended to be a poem in its own right, as 'a tale of other days' and adds that 'the man whom I copy has been dead for nearly a century . . . his character floats in the memory of the village – & from that my resources are gleaned'. 'The Vicar' obviously owes something to Goldsmith's preacher, 'A man . . . to all the country dear/And passing rich with forty pounds a year', and to Crabbe's *Tales of the Hall* (1819). Clare sets out at least to emulate these poets, but in the end makes what was to be a separate study part of a section in which he contrasts old and present times in the village (11. 1584–963). This picks up many of the issues to which Howkins's and

Dyck's essay draws attention. In both *The Parish* and *The Shepherd's Calendar* – and there must be considerable overlap in the writing of the two poems – Clare notes how old-style farmers 'used their servants toils to share', whereas Farmer Thrifty, who sounds very like the Clares' landlord, not only took pains to separate himself from his workers but 'raised their rents and bid their hopes depart'. Howkins and Dyck point out that 'My Old Hat' points to a 'recent change . . . from one way of ordering work and working life to another . . . Central to the old order was social harmony . . . symbolised by the similarities of behaviour and dress. Yet it was not an equal society . . . rather it was one in which men were bound together by their "words" into a society of mutuality.' The nature of this change is taken up in *The Parish*, and that Clare isn't indulging an unfocused nostalgia, let alone a dream of an egalitarian past, can be seen from the evidence of Edward Butt, given to the Poor Law Commission in 1837, and quoted by Howkins and Dyck.

> My father was a farmer, and I was always with [the labouring poor] . . . when I was young I used to have meals with them, and go out to work with them, and the people of the house used to have their fat pork and such things, to live upon in the house . . . [The labourers] used to come in at their meal time, at dinner time, and bring their bit of bread and pork in their hand . . . and sit down by the fire and take their small beer.

This is very close to several passages in *The Parish* which have an understanding of ways in a village not to be looked for in Goldsmith's fine poem. Nor could Goldsmith have written anything like the closing lines of 'June', in *The Shepherd's Calendar*, where Clare writes of past times

> When masters made them merry wi' their men
> Whose coat was like his neighbours russet brown
> And whose rude speech was vulgar as his clown
> Who in the same horn drank the rest among
> And joined the chorus while a labourer sung

We can assume that the 'plain old farmer and the neighbouring poor' of *The Parish* (line 1653) all wear 'russet brown', and this colour had a deep resonance for Clare. In *The Parish* itself he remarks that 'satires muse puts on a russet gown', meaning that he will take the point of view of the common people; and russet brown is the colour of favourite song-birds, including the robin and nightingale. It implies, then, *community*. Howkins and Dyck note that in certain ballads 'the linsey-woolsey gown (cheap plain cloth made of wool and flax) has a recurring and powerful significance as a symbol of plainness, neatness and hard work'. And commonly worn dress implies work done in common, whereas new fashions, such as Farmer Thrifty in *The Parish* takes care to follow, imply separation: of rich from poor, the empowered from the disempowered. This is close to a moment in 'The Widow's Tale', one of Crabbe's *Tales in Verse* (1812), where Farmer Moss's daughter, who has been sent to the city to finish her education, is appalled on her return to the farm where she grew up to find that she is expected to eat with her father and his men in the kitchen.

> When the coarse cloth she saw, with many a stain,
> Soil'd by rude hinds who cut and came again,
> She could not breathe, but with a heavy sigh
> Rein'd the fair neck and shut th' offended eye;
> She minced the sanguine flesh in frustums fine,
> And wonder'd much to see the creatures dine.

Crabbe's poem here points a moment of separation that is part of the history of class relations. For Clare, the separation is however more acutely felt. The well dressed are now visibly different from those who are dressed in 'rags' and who therefore come near to that condition of nakedness which, as we have seen, he always thinks of as a stripping away of all dignity and worth.

Those who are reduced to rags become the objects of fashionable scorn. And scorn shows on faces and in the behaviour of those who administer the new poor law and its most obvious and degrading physical fact, the workhouse. The ragged are 'Shoved as a nusiance from pride's scornfull sight'. 'Scorn frownd and placd them on the sunless side' (11. 1788 and 1807). For agricultural workers 'the primacy of agricultural production gives men and women who work in agriculture a special place: they are not "beggars at the door" or "thieves" to be scorned, but the children of Adam supporting the entire social order'. Thus Howkins and Dyck. Clare would have agreed, but *The Parish*, as with much else of his work, is about the fact that agricultural labourers *have* been reduced to objects of scorn. And even though in a magnificent passage he imagines how one such scorner will go down to his grave where 'His power wastes all to nothingness away/As showers at night wash out the steps of day' (11. 2050–1), the fact remains that the scorn of the powerful rips away the dignity of those they have made poor. That Clare should on occasion seem to be one of the scorners goes far to explain why he could never finish *The Parish* to his satisfaction. He admits as much in his preface. He must have written this when he was trying to persuade himself that for all its changeableness, the different parts of the poem somehow hung together.

> This poem was begun & finished under the pressure of heavy distress with embittred feelings under a state of anxiety & oppression almost amounting to slavery – when the prosperity of one class was founded on the adversity & distress of the other – The haughty demand by the master to his labourer was work for the little I chuse to alow you & go to the parish for the rest – or starve – to decline working under such advantages was next to offending a magistrate & no oppertunity was lost in marking the insult by some unquallified oppression – but better times & better prospects have opened a peace establishment of more sociable feeling & kindness – & to no one upon earth do I owe ill will

In his edition of *The Parish* Eric Robinson remarks that the final section of the preface 'is never quoted and so the reader is left with a more severe impression than Clare intended'. But Clare is trying to cover up for the anger which fuels much of the writing in his poem. Either that, or he is apologizing to his presumed audience of 'polite' readers – the only readers he had. He may of course have hoped for better times and prospects for himself, but his poem repeatedly shows that for the villagers of Helpston the times and prospects were getting worse. 'Sociable feeling and kindness' could be a way of registering the intentions of philanthropic evangelicanism, but the phrase reveals that, in not writing *for* the community he is writing *about*, Clare is acutely conscious of a huge and perhaps irresolvable problem: how to mediate between the two in a way that won't distort the real truth of village life by turning it into a simplified 'literary' image for ready consumption by his readers. Given that this image includes the linguistic traps of such terms as 'peasant' and 'clown' – with all that they imply about 'unlettered' innocence – it's inevitable that Clare should occasionally fail.

It is also inevitable that in some poems he should strike a literary pose. Hence, for example, the opening of 'Summer Images', with its Thomson-like 'Miltonics'. 'Now swathy summer by rude health embrowned/Presedence takes of rosey fingered spring . . . Then with thy sultry locks all loose and rude/And mantle laced with gems of garish light/Come as of wont for I would fain intrude . . .' Once he gets into the poem Clare by and large abandons this language, but he doesn't let go of the pose of pastoral poet, hymning a free nature. 'I love to walk the fields they are to me/A legacy no evil can destroy', he says towards the end; and you feel, yes, but they *have* been destroyed. Clare's pose here is as phoney as in the preceding stanza, which is draped in the tushery of literary pastoral he so loathed: 'soothing calm', 'meek eyed moods', 'balmy trills', 'dreamy eve'. This is the language of the 'rural muse', and it is perhaps no wonder that the poem should have been included in the 1835 collection of that title.

By the same token it should come as no surprise that 'The Progress of Rhyme' was never published in Clare's lifetime. This lovely poem, with its seemingly inexhaustible rush of octosyllabic couplets, celebrates Clare's commitment to descriptive verse and to the particularity which is at once of things seen, heard and known through names. His insistence on a 'right to song' in some ways recalls 'The Village Minstrel', but this poem is more candidly auto-biographical; and its loving concern for a world of 'little things', of flowers and birds, anticipates much that will go into *The Shepherd's Calendar*. In particular lines 229–60, which describe the nightingale's various songs, are miracles of exact observation and onomatopoeic resourcefulness. Too long to quote, the passage is quintessential Clare, above all in its unabashed celebration of the natural world which is also, and separately, a celebration of his ability to write such poetry – an ability that has never been equalled. No one else can write like this.

But joy in his answerable powers is set against a feeling that the likes of him had no claim to poetry. It was 'A title that I dared not name/And hid it like a private shame . . . /I dreaded laughter more then blame/And dared not sing aloud for shame'. There is a degree of self-doubt here that needs to be taken seriously because Clare keeps returning to it: to being 'A clownish silent haynish boy/Who even felt ashamed of joy' and who then moves, very significantly, from the sense of his unfitness for the title of poet to his awareness of Mary Joyce: 'thou whose very name/I loved whose look was even

47

fame'; She is somehow linked to the questionable right to song, to guilty love, or to that more social sense of 'shame'; and this becomes obsessive and a matter he returns to in a very late, beautiful poem, 'I hid my love'. It's as though his most powerful positive emotions are also the ones that cause him greatest unease. Mary becomes a symbol for his love of poetry and of place, and he feels his hold on and right to both are tenuous. Given the loss of 'labours rights' and the identification of poets with print culture this isn't surprising. Very deep in Clare's psyche there lurks a confusion about his entitlement to being 'The poet in his joy'. It is his 'shame' (the word which Johnson glossed as 'the passion supposed to be felt when reputation is lost'.) 'Shame' points as well as any other term to the malign dilemma with which Clare had to live. What's so wonderful about him is that his poetry nevertheless testifies to resources which are still deeper and more compelling.

But Clare's imagination is increasingly seized by images of vulnerability. It's at this time that he begins to write his great poems about birds, a subject that would preoccupy him for a number of years. In fact, once he'd found it, it never really went away. It's given early, memorable expression in the poem 'To the Snipe', written in 1824.

> Lover of swamps
> The quagmire overthrown
> With hassock tufts of sedge – where fear encamps
> Around thy home alone
>
> The trembling grass
> Quakes from the human foot
> Nor bears the weight of man to let him pass
> Where he alone and mute
>
> Sitteth at rest
> In safety near the clump
> of hugh flag-forrest that thy haunts invest
> Or some old sallow stump . . .

The unusual stanza structure of this shows that Clare is well aware of that convention of odes to birds associated with Wordsworth and Shelley (and wonderfully satirized in the *The Pickwick Papers*, in Mrs Leo Hunter's 'Ode to an Expiring Frog'). But unlike them, Clare's 'lover of swamps' is no blithe spirit. Instead, 'fear encamps/Around thy home alone'; it is a guardian who sits 'at rest' only in a place that's beyond human intrusive force. And where Wordsworth speaks of the cuckoo as a 'blessed bird', whose song suggests that 'the earth we pace/Again appears to be/An unsubstantial faery place', Clare recognizes that the snipe's survival depends on the fact that only in 'the dreariest places' will peace be 'a dweller and a joy'. The substantial earth is elsewhere the property of those who threaten the snipe's very existence. Even dwelling – that key Wordsworthian term for rootedness, deep commitment to place – becomes impossible except on the margins.

'To the Snipe' provides an insight, a 'reading' of the vulnerability of natural life, repeated in 'Sand Martin'. Here, Clare watches the bird

> Flirting about the unfrequented sky
> And felt a feeling that I cant describe
> Of lone seclusion and a hermit joy
> To see thee circle round nor go beyond
> That lone heath and its melancholy pond

'Circle round' both describes an arc of joyous activity and its strict limits. Only here, in an 'unfrequented' sky above the 'lone' heath, is the bird safe. In his 'hermit joy' Clare shares a secret delight with the bird's 'flirting' – the word beautifully catching the bird's glad, ripply, almost skittish, movement, its assertion of what might be called a right to song. But the word also hints that such rights are asserted despite great risks, as one flirts with danger.

I don't at all wish to imply that for Clare the birds about which he writes so wonderfully are merely metaphors for his own condition. That would be to insult the exactness of his writing about them, the loving care with which he records their nests, eggs, calls, habitats. But it is to say that he is compulsively drawn to recognize that, as he notes of the green woodpecker, it seeks out habitation 'Far from the sight of troubling man'; and in this he is a long way from Wordsworth's eager identification with the cuckoo's 'wandering voice', with its suggestion of the endless freedom Wordsworth could claim for himself as poet. Freedom for Clare is altogether more fugitive, secret, is a hidden or hermit joy.

The lines about the green woodpecker come from 'May' in *The*

Shepherd's Calendar. The Parish may be a mess. Not so this other long poem. It was, however, badly messed about by Taylor. He himself had suggested the idea to Clare, in a letter of August 1823, and Clare was so taken with it that early the following year the poem was being advertised for publication. But although Clare received his first proofs in March 1825, *The Shepherd's Calendar* was not published for a further two years, and when it finally saw the light of day it sold poorly. Only 400 copies had gone by the end of 1829. Whether its disappointing sales owed very much to the publisher's extraordinary editorial behaviour I doubt; by the later years of the 1820s the vogue for poetry, and especially 'peasant poetry', was largely over. But Taylor can't have helped. True, he had his own problems. By now he had found that he lacked the skills to make the *London Magazine* required reading; he was short of cash; and he was about to decide to give up publishing any poetry. Poetry didn't pay. Add to this what I think must have been his desire to make Clare conform not just to being a peasant poet but to 'refined taste' and it's obvious that the manuscript Clare handed him spelt trouble.

It certainly couldn't appeal to such taste. Dugald Stewart, an important arbiter in these matters, had restated a commonplace when he claimed that 'certain objects are fitted to give pleasure, and others disgust', and that 'we know [this] from experience alone'. Understanding of this 'fittedness' marks, Stewart says, 'the progress of taste, from rudeness to refinement'. 'We' readers of poetry are clearly the refined. Reviews of Clare's earlier work had jibbed at his 'rudeness', which was tantamount to remarking that he hadn't a sure sense of 'fit' objects of pleasure. Nor had he. As Robinson and Summerfield point out in the introduction to their edition of *The Shepherd's Calendar*, Taylor cancelled Clare's reference to 'smell smocks' 'because he disliked the country name for a lecher'. He would have had considerations of refined taste in mind there as he would when he knocked out the description of fairies crowding in cupboards, 'As thick as mites in rotten cheese'. There are many other such instances of Taylor's blue pencil. 'Artificial delicacy' Robinson and Summerfield call it, by way of accusing Clare's publisher of being as bad in this respect as Radstock. No doubt. But Taylor's 'taste' was neither better nor worse than most of his readers'. That is why he tidied up the poem's grammar and mended its punctuation; and why he altered or got rid of many local and dialect words. It is why he told Clare that 'your Poetry is much the best when you are not describing

50

common things, and if you would raise your Views generally, &
speak of the Appearances of Nature each Month more philoso-
phically . . . or with more Excitement, you would greatly improve
these little poems'. And it is why virtually half the poem Clare
submitted to him was cut from the published version.

Yet Clare's original is a great poem. The only month that isn't up
to much is 'April', which comes closest to following Taylor's
prescriptions ('Sweet month thy pleasure bids thee be/The fairest
child of spring'). But at its greatest – which it frequently is – the
poem is both celebratory and elegiac, and with a freshness, a vivid
concern for 'custom', which is unique in English poetry.

> Old customs O I love the sound
> However simple they may be
> What ere wi time has sanction found
> Is welcome and is dear to me
> Pride grows above simplicity
> And spurns it from her haughty mind
> And soon the poets song will be
> The only refuge they can find

This stanza from 'December' recalls Wordsworth's claim in the
Preface to *The Lyrical Ballads* that the poet functions at least partly
as historian, to keep hold of 'things silently gone out of mind and
things violently destroyed'. It is noticeable that even when he
celebrates old customs Clare feels required to apologize for their
'simplicity'. And yet the poem as a whole shows that the customs
are anything but simple. Each month provides the chance for an
exuberant catalogue in which nothing is granted superiority over
anything else, and the rolling, catch-all syntax – and . . . and . . . and
. . . – itemizes and rejoices in everything that's recalled. 'January: A
Cottage Evening' recounts folk tales and local histories; 'March'
is about work: hedger, ditcher, ploughman, sower, driving boy,
shepherd's boy, all active now that 'Days lengthen in their visits a
"cocks stride" '. Then comes the sequence of spring, summer and
autumn months, where the poem's most dazzling writing is to be
found.

In a letter to Hessey, dated July 1823, Clare remarks that 'Hazlitt
says, the early writers described flowers the best; perhaps they
do'. He then reveals something of his formidable knowledge of

Shakespeare, Milton, Cowley and 'my favourite Thomson', as poets who have written well about flowers, although even Thomson 'is mistaken about the Cowslip, as it is a very favoured flower, and no cottager's garden is without it, nor the farmer's neither'. 'All spring flowers are beloved with us', he goes on, 'but the summer ones seem hardly to claim any notice, their names are lost in their number'. The letter reads like a rehearsal for that section of 'May' where, as he says, 'My wild field catalogue of flowers/Grows in my ryhmes as thick as showers'. It does, too, although the octosyllabic couplets are still more like a prolonged drench of names, colours, lore.

> And scarlet starry points of flowers
> Pimpernel dreading nights and showers
> Oft calld 'the shepherds weather glass'
> That sleep til suns have dyd the grass
> Then wakes and spreads its creeping bloom
> Till clouds or threatening shadows come
> Then close it shuts to sleep again
> Which weeders see and talk of rain
> And boys that mark them shut so soon
> Will call them 'John go bed at noon'

A passage such as this provides the hint for what Edward Thomas, who loved Clare, would pick up and develop in his great poem 'Lob'. Names, lore, local voices surviving in phrase are threaded together to form a peopled history, a field full of folk.

Some years after Clare's wonderful and entirely unique poem was written, Ruskin, who as far as I know was unaware of Clare's existence, advised young artists to go to nature, 'rejecting nothing, selecting nothing, and scorning nothing'. More than any other poem I know, *The Shepherd's Calendar* bears out Ruskin's prescription. To quote from it is practically impossible, without at least quoting at length, precisely because Clare refuses to reject or scorn, and because he won't select, either – that is, won't rank or make a hierarchy of customs, flora and fauna. The teeming activity of his lines democratizes all it gathers up, whether he is talking about the wild flowers and birds of 'May', the games of 'June', the daily working routines of 'July', or the harvesting of 'September'.

It is of course possible to suggest that *The Shepherd's Calendar* is hurt by Clare's nostalgic love for what he presents as a lost contentment. This indeed is what Merryn and Raymond Williams imply when they say that 'There was no fall from Eden, but rather a new phase of the long conquest and repression of working country people by wave after wave of landlords and masters'. They have in mind the enclosure which, at the end of 'May', Clare refers to as spreading a mildew over the land and which, in 'October', is invoked when he describes 'the sticking groups' who glean faggots 'On commons where no farmers claims appear/Nor tyrant justice rides to interfere'. But what the Williamses overlook or have no way of accounting for are those resources of joy to which I have repeatedly drawn attention because Clare repeatedly draws attention to them. Not to register the exuberance, the unabashed, loving delight that goes into his celebration of custom – of customs in common – is to make him into an altogether different and lesser poet. That he should have to identify such custom as belonging to a past out of reach except to memory is certainly tragic: but it is so because of what he understands as a radical dislocation, a severance between then and now. *His* experience is what we should be concerned with, not some historical gloss which diminishes the actuality of his poetry and makes it dully 'representative', when it is in fact unique and uniquely valuable.

5

'Chances Way'

In the years following the disappointments over the publication and sales of *The Shepherd's Calendar* Clare became increasingly bitter. When in the spring of 1831 he read Southey's *Lives of Uneducated Poets*, which had appeared in 1830, he wrote angrily to Taylor to tell him that 'Mr Southey seems to hold uneducated poets in very little estimation & talks about the march of mind in a sneering way'. This is perhaps less than fair to a work which, whatever its failings, does its best to provide a sympathetic account of a number of insufficiently regarded poets. Unfortunately, Clare was not listed among them. Hence, no doubt, his anger. Reading through Southey's book he must have feared he was becoming invisible, and this same fear can be felt behind a letter he sent to Taylor later in 1831, in which he says that he needs stimulus and encouraging inspiration. 'But I live in a land overflowing with obscurity and vulgarity far away from taste & books & friends'. The point of this letter is to ask his publisher if he will agree to take another collection of poems.

Clare still yearned for reputation and money from print. Then 'I shall become an independent man & care for nobody but friends'. He had formed a plan, to move from the cottage in Helpston to one in the village of Northborough, some three miles off. There, he would be able to write, and with sales of garden produce he would make enough to be truly 'independent'. The independence Clare has in mind is as much social as financial. No more patrons, no more subservience, no more bending to the tastes of others. And no more truck with obscurity and vulgarity.

A Man of Independent Means. It is a dream of freedom which, even as he spoke of his continuing hopes, Clare must have sensed was probably beyond him. In 1830 he was taken to the theatre at Peterborough to see a performance of *The Merchant of Venice* and in the trial scene became so incensed by Shylock's demanding his pound of flesh that he shouted at the actor and had to be bundled out of the theatre. It isn't difficult to see in this irrational behaviour a hint of his maddened sense of lawless laws operating to destroy freedom. In the same year he produced a great sonnet, 'England 1830', which, needless to say, was never published in his lifetime.

> These vague allusions to a country's wrong,
>   Where one says 'Ay' and others answer 'No'
> In contradiction from a thousand tongues,
>   Till like to prison-cells her freedoms grow
> Becobwebbed with these oft-repeated songs
>   Of peace and plenty in the midst of woe –
> And is it thus they mock her year by year
> Telling poor truth unto her face she lies,
> Declaiming of her wealth with gibe severe,
>   So long as taxes drain their wished supplies?
> And will these jailers rivet every chain
>   Anew, yet loudest in their mockery be,
> To damn her into madness with disdain,
>   Forging new bonds and bidding her be free?

Well, will they? The question seems rhetorical. Those who have social power – the scorners/disdainers – are also the upholders of tyrant justice, for whom there is indeed peace and plenty in the midst of woe. There was no shortage of wealth among the farmers in the late 1820s, nor, as Corrigan and Sayer remind us, of laws to maintain and increase their wealth. But chains can be broken, prisons opened. 1830 was the year of the Swing riots and it is possible, and I would say even necessary, to read the ending of Clare's sonnet as holding out a defiant answer to the mocking jailers.

The previous year Clare had readily welcomed the chance to write for John Drakard's new radical paper, the *Stamford Champion*. It was a good moment for Drakard to risk the venture. In the late 1820s a considerable number of radical papers came into existence, at both local and national levels. The best known was Cobbett's *Twopenny Trash*, but there were many others, including the *Ballot*, the *Voice of the People* and Richard Carlile's the *Prompter*. As these titles imply, the issue of the proposed new franchise was one of the papers' major concerns. So were the Corn Laws. Halévy remarks that 'all these papers if they did not directly incite the agricultural labourer to burn mills and break machines excused acts of disorder'.

With this in mind we can better understand the impulse behind some letters that Clare at this time sent to Marianne Marsh, wife of the bishop of Peterborough. On 6 July 1831, he apologizes for not having returned a book she had lent him, but excuses himself on the grounds that the previous winter 'it was dangerous for any lone person to go even a journey to Peterboro – such was the state of feeling among that useful but ignorant class of people our peasantry that mischief became so predominant & daring as to threaten the peacable even in their cottages & I hope for the sake of my own feelings never to see such another threatening winter again – for I fear there is even in our day a class of desperadoes little or no better than the rabble that made up the army of Jack Cade'. This goes in opposed directions. On the one hand, there is the deep sympathy he has with 'our' peasants. On the other, they are a 'rabble'. Given his correspondent, these contradictory statements should come as no surprise. As so often, Clare is trying to separate himself from his own deepest commitments.

Or is he? He does also seem to be genuine in his effort to make Marianne Marsh understand why violence has broken out. And so he tells her that although 'the mob' possesses only 'brute strength' and are 'so many savages', 'I am sorry to say they had too much apology for joining such disturbances as their wants had been so long neglected as to be entirely forgotten until it burst out into the terrible jepordays' – and these, he concludes, 'were the chief reasons for my keeping this book so long'. Or, as we might reasonably think, the book becomes a good excuse for the Ranters' friend to explain to the wife of the bishop of Peterborough the poverty and destitution of agricultural workers in her husband's see, and to justify the resultant rick-burning and wrecking of threshing-machines. In their definitive study, *Captain Swing*, Hobsbawm and Rudé show how, during the autumn 1830, these spread rapidly across the counties of Bedford, Huntingdon, Cambridge and Northampton. And this is the period to which Clare refers in his letter.

The following January he writes to Marianne Marsh again. He looks on Cobbett, he now tells her, as 'one of the most powerful prose writers of the age – with no principles to make those powers commendable to honest praise'. Cobbett apparently uses arguments which contain 'too much of party colouring'. What Clare desires is a reform, but 'not the reform of mobs where the bettering of the many is only an apology for injuring the few – nor the reform of party's where the benefits of one is the destruction of the other but a reform that would do good & hurt none'. Clare probably means most of this. After all, he was excluded from party interest simply because he had no vote. (The Reform Bill, about to be acted upon, extended the franchise only to those whose freehold property could be reckoned as worth at least £10 rental a year.) Besides, among 'the few' were people like Marianne Marsh herself who had done him real kindnesses. But if this letter – the gist of which is repeated in a fragment of an essay – is intended to position him as a man of independence, it runs up against the fact that his move to North-borough quite failed to bring him the independence for which he hoped. Not only did he leave Helpston owing back-rent, but shortly after he arrived at his new abode he was stirred to fury by a report in the *Athenaeum* that the cottage had been given him as an act of charity. 'It troubles me & injures my feeling of a propriety of independence', he protested to Taylor. He was soon to be dealt a more insulting injury still.

Clare had been gathering his poems together for another collection which was to be called *The Midsummer Cushion*. The title alludes to a custom, then common in Northamptonshire, in which cottagers would gather field and hedge flowers, arrange them on a bed of moss, and so decorate windowsill or table. Clare had been writing poems about the flora of his local county; he had also been writing a vast number of poems about birds' nests. Among those that would find their way into the volume when it appeared in 1835 was 'The Pettichaps Nest' – pettichaps being the local name for willow-warbler. The poem opens in a manner reminiscent of Coleridge's 'conversation' poem 'This Lime-Tree Bower My Prison'. 'Well, they are gone and here I must remain'. That is Coleridge, and this is Clare. 'Well in my many walks I rarely found/A place less likely for a bird to form'. But as with Coleridge, so Clare's poem can be thought of as less conversation than monologue. True, he insists that he has company on his walk. When he speaks of the nest, he says that 'you and I/Had surely passed it in our walk to day/Had chance not led us by it . . .' And later, having found some eggs, he remarks, 'We'll let them be'. But this seems all too obviously the stratagem of someone trying momentarily to break out of an enclosing, isolated world, which the poem as a whole takes for granted, even takes as refuge. This is at one with the poet's happenstance discovery of the bird itself: it reinforces an atmosphere of secrecy, elusiveness.

> – Stop heres the bird that woodman at the gap
> Hath frit it from the hedge – tis olive green
> Well I declare it is the pettichaps
> Not bigger then the wren and seldom seen
> Ive often found their nests in chances way
> But never did I dream until today
> A spot like this would be her chosen home

Delighted discovery, here as elsewhere in the bird poems of this period, is poised against a sense of threatening forces, always felt if not always seen. To take one example: Clare's 'The Sky Lark', unlike Shelley's, is a bird seeking safety from what 'may come at to destroy'. Clare associates the lark with the hare which squats 'to terrors wide awake/Like some brown clod the harrows failed to break'. At the poem's end the bird in 'its low nest moist with the dews of morn/Lies safely with the leveret in the corn'. But such safety is at best temporary. Come the harvest and the grown hare will be trapped and killed as it runs for safety from the encircling reapers. Clare doesn't say this, but then he doesn't need to. He would take for granted his readers' knowledge of the hare's fate.

To repeat a point already made, neither hare nor lark – nor pettichaps – is a metaphor for the poet. Clare is an unrivalled observer and describer of flora and fauna, of things in themselves. Nevertheless, he is increasingly drawn to recognize the vulnerable frailty of the world of little things, as though his own predicament, isolation, sense of hurt, direct him to such frailty. It is therefore significant that in 'The Sky Lark' the hare's protective colouring should be described as that of the earth's 'russet clods'. I have noted that in earlier poems Clare had always identified 'russet brown' with the familiar, customary, with work and habitation. Now, these are themselves under threat.

> up the sky lark flies
> & oer her half formed nest with happy wings
> Winnows the air – till in the cloud she sings
> Then hangs a dust spot in the sunny skies
> & drops & drops till in her nest she lies
> Where boys unheeding past

Joy is fugitive. In 'Remembrances', a most beautiful poem of this period, Clare similarly focuses on the vulnerability of little things, in this case the moles, or 'mouldiwarps'. 'Here was commons for their hills where they seek for freedom still/Though every commons gone and though traps are set to kill/The little homeless miners'. The poem's skipping, lilting stresses, like a broadside ballad, attempt to breathe cadences of joy into a burden which is gripped by a tragic sense of loss. 'Summer pleasures they are gone like to visions every one', the poem starts, but though the visions are summoned up, they are isolated in a past which can be recaptured only through memory, now that, as the sudden shift from anapaest to the heavy, insistent stresses of iambics imply

> Inclosure like a Buonaparte let not a thing remain
> It levelled every bush and tree and levelled every hill
> And hung the moles for traitors – though the brook is running still
> It runs a naked brook cold and chill

Clare uses a final short line, roughly iambic pentameter, to bring each of the poem's eight ten-line stanzas to a close; and the effect is to break the ballad cadences, to enforce a sense of dislocation between past and present. The last lines utter a grievous sense of loss, isolation, betrayal, or, as here, the indignity of the 'naked'.

It is therefore relevant to note that 'Remembrances' was written after the move to Northborough. So was 'The Flitting', which I am reasonably sure is one of the great poems of the nineteenth century. It speaks for and from a radical disorientation which isn't simply to be explained in terms of that three-mile gap between Helpston and Clare's new home, even if that is what at first the poem seems to be saying.

> Ive left my own old home of homes
> Green fields and every pleasant place
> The summer like a stranger comes
> I pause and hardly know her face . . .
>
> I sit me in my corner chair
> That seems to feel itself from home
> I hear bird music here and there
> From awthorn hedge and orchard come
> I hear but all is strange and new . . .

I walk adown the narrow lane
The nightingale is singing now
But like to me she seems at loss
For royce wood and its shielding bough
I lean upon the window sill
The trees and summer happy seem
Green sunny green they shine – but still
My heart goes far away to dream

Of happiness and thoughts arise
With home bred pictures many a one
Green lanes that shut out burning skies
And old crooked stiles to rest upon
Above them hangs the maple tree
Below grass swells a velvet hill
And little footpads sweet to see
Goes seeking sweeter places still

The poem starts from loss, strangeness. Then memory takes hold, and as it does so the past becomes the present. You can feel the eager, darting way Clare looks around, above, below. And it is characteristic that his vision should briefly come to rest with that 'velvet hill', for molehills have a special place in his poetry: themselves tiny homes, they testify to the 'secret' ways of natural phenomena and provide welcoming seats from which he can survey his landscape. They are part of a rich natural economy, and their occupants' footpads lead to an elusive Edenic world of 'sweeter places still'. But he has to carry all this in his mind. For he is now 'Alone and in a stranger scene'. This is literally untrue, of course. He had gone to Northborough with his family. But the isolation he feels is an expression of that disorientation or alienation from any secure sense of self which the move triggered and which brought with it an aggrieved recognition that the world of literary fashion had left him behind.

For books they follow fashions new
And throw all old esteems away
In crowded streets flowers never grew
But many there hath died away

He's thinking of himself there, and of Byron when he goes on to say that 'Some sing the pomps of chivalry'. But true sublimity belongs to 'plain and simpler things'

> And David underneath a tree
> Sought when a shepherd Salems springs

> Where moss did unto cushions spring
> Forming a seat of velvet hue
> A small unnoticed trifling thing
> To all but heavens daily dew
> And Davids crown hath passed away
> Yet poesy breaths his shepherd-skill
> His palace lost – and to this day
> The little moss is blooming still

It would be easy to underestimate the importance of these lines. Clare is saying not merely that true poetry is 'nature' poetry, but that it has its roots in ordinary living, the lives of commoners. 'Salems springs' can after all be linked not merely to the life of the fields but to the sermons of the radical Methodists who spoke to and for the people. (In *The Parish* Clare had said that 'The Ranter priests that take the street to teach/Swears god builds churches where so ere they preach', 11. 535–6.) Methodist chapels were often named 'Salem'. And for all that the power of the city, of thrones and palaces, endlessly threatens to overwhelm the people, the palace will finally crumble whereas 'the little moss is blooming still'. For this poem of 1832, though aware of the limitations of the Reform Act, also breathes the recent defiance of the Swing rioters.

And having once got to this point, this sense of defiant communality, Clare keeps returning to it. Weeds and grasses, those unimportant and even unwelcome intruders in the well-weeded fields and gardens of enclosure, nevertheless persist. Later in this poem, one that only gradually unfolds its complexities as Clare searches his way into them, he will say that 'I feel at times a love and joy/For every weed', and that the 'shepherds purse' is 'an ancient neighbour'. And then, recalling how he was free to wander about the country of his boyhood, he remembers how 'every weed and blossom too/Was looking upward in my face/With friendships welcome "how do ye do" '. We must remember that the term 'weed' has no botanical meaning. A weed is simply the name given to any plant that is not wanted. There is a thread connecting the familiar name 'shepherd's purse' to David the shepherd, to poetry and its rightful concern 'Amid such neighbourhoods to dwell' as the ones he knows best, those customary neighbourhoods of friendship and familiar talk from which he has been doubly exiled: by the lure of print culture and by acts of enclosure.

The poem's final lines gather up all the issues raised in the previous twenty-six stanzas.

> Time looks on pomp with careless moods
> Or killing apathys disdain
> – So where old marble citys stood
> Poor persecuted weeds remain
> She feels a love for little things
> That very few can feel beside
> And still the grass eternal springs
> Where castles stood and grandeur died

It had become almost a commonplace by the 1830s to identity the plebs with grass. The more you cut it down the more it sprang back up. There was also a developing commonplace about what the French writer Volney had in the 1790s dubbed *The Ruins of Empire*. So in England Cowper had spoken in *The Task* of how once-mighty kingdoms, built 'With what we deem eternal rock', will nevertheless crumble to dust; and this sense of Time as destroyer had of course prompted Shelley's sonnet 'Ozymandias', although he makes Time point the vanity of the tyrant's ambition. That, too, will turn to a desert of uniformity. Clare brings the two commonplaces together at the close of his great poem, not in order to mourn the passing of all things or merely to condemn the vanity of worldly power (though he must have enjoyed turning Time's disdain against the worldly scorners who had no time for him); overriding these matters is his exultant insistence on the 'grass eternal' as an invading army which will finally overwhelm its apparently irresistible enemies. The careful positioning of 'springs' affirms a continuous and ultimately victorious energy of opposition to castles and grandeur.

'The Flitting', like 'The Sky Lark', was included in the collection which was finally published in 1835 – the last volume of Clare's poems to be published in his lifetime. 'Remembrances', however, was less lucky. Together with up to half the poems Clare had hoped to include, it was dropped. The responsibility for this rests with Mrs Emmerson and her husband, who had agreed to 'edit' Clare's poems for the London firm of Whitaker's. (Taylor had kept to his intention of publishing no more poetry.) The Emmersons not only left out some of Clare's finest poems, they re-wrote, re-punctuated, refashioned. They also rejected the fresh, unusual and idiomatic title Clare had chosen. Instead, a volume which, despite its omissions, remains a great collection of poems, was sent out into the world under the stalest, most sentimental of titles, *The Rural Muse*.

6

'Fear of the Foe'

The Rural Muse was generously reviewed, but its poor sales did nothing to improve Clare's spirits. During the summer of 1835 he seems to have suffered from a depression so acute that we would nowadays be likely to call it breakdown. In August of that year he wrote to a doctor who had previously advised him, to tell him that 'I am very unwell . . . sounds affect me very much & things evil as well as good thoughts are continually rising in my mind I cannot sleep for I am asleep as it were with my eyes open & feel chills come over me & a great sort of nightmare awake . . .' His condition didn't prevent him from writing – hardly anything could do that; but the poems of this period offer a clue to his condition. A series of ballads and songs about Mary Joyce all turn on the conviction that she is his 'true' wife. Some of them eventually find their way into a loose sequence of poems to which he will give the title *Child Harold*. And at the same time he plans another long poem, to be called *Don Juan*. Put these together and it becomes apparent that Clare is imagining himself into an alternate identity: the successful lover of a socially superior woman and also the most famous poet of the age.

It is, then, very significant that other poems of this period are marked by a dark brutality in which birds and animals are presented as victims of violence and persecution. The sonnet on 'The Puddock's Nest' ends:

> The schoolboy often hears the old ones cry
> And climbs the tree and gets them ere they fly
> And takes them home and often cuts their wing
> And ties them in a garden with a string.

Other bird poems echo the flat, insistent tone of these lines, con-centrate on moments of distress, suffering, maiming, the wrecking of nests. They may seem to recall a famous episode in Book I of *The Prelude*, where Wordsworth remembers how, as a boy, he ensnared birds

> and when the deed was done
> I heard among the solitary hills
> Low breathings coming after me, and sounds
> Of undistinguishable motion, steps
> Almost as silent as the turf they trod
>
> (11. 328–32)

Clare couldn't have known these lines, because *The Prelude* was not published until 1850. But anyway his concern is different from Wordsworth's. Wordsworth's lines are prompted by an intensely protestant imagination, in which a personal – and minatory – god makes his presence literally felt through nature and drives the conscience back on itself. This was why Wordsworth could say 'fair seed-time had my soul' and recall how he grew up 'Fostered alike by beauty and by fear'. It is an aspect of the Egotistical Sublime. Clare, on the other hand, is not concerned with the conscience and consciousness of the schoolboy but with his *victims*: his empathy with a world of little things is in utter opposition to Wordsworth's almost obsessive self-regard.

And now it leads him to sense cruelty everywhere. The double sonnet 'The Marten' speaks of how the animal 'hurrys through the woodland gaps / And poachers shoot and make his skin for caps'. In another double sonnet, Clare writes of the fox, hunted by the ploughman who 'laughed and would have ploughed him in / But the old shepherd took him for the skin'. The fox finally escapes, but not before 'The ploughman beat him till his skin would crack'. As for 'The Hedgehog':

> But still they hunt the hedges all about
> And shepherd dogs are trained to hunt them out
> They hurl with savage force the stick and stone
> And no one cares and still the strife goes on

Here, 'they' operate like the mindless crowd which Auden identified as the feared mass of many of Edward Lear's limericks. 'They' may, then, seem similar to the unindividuated crowd of much Romantic

65

poetry (the Londoners in Book VII of *The Prelude*, the Ancient Mariner's shipmates). But again there is a difference. In all these cases 'they' oppose the isolated individual, who is therefore granted a special status. True, this can include the status of victim, but that only serves to emphasize the individual's heroic apartness. The victims of Clare's poems, on the other hand, are helpless, non-heroic. Nothing dignifies them. Hence, 'The Badger' who

> falls as dead and kicked by boys and men
> Then starts and grins and drives the crowd agen
> Till kicked and torn and beaten out he lies
> And leaves his hold and cackles groans and dies

These lines bring to a close the fourth stanza of five, in each of which Clare details the badger's sufferings, its being baited, beaten, its resistence, its further suffering. The tone feels almost reportorial, the language peculiarly stark, stripped of adjectives. Verbs command our attention. Twelve of them in four lines, following each other in pitiless sequence. In earlier poems birds had found strategies for survival no matter how precarious. But now they and the badger, fox, hedgehog, mole are hunted down and destroyed, along with their dwelling places.

All of the poems mentioned were written between 1835 and 1837. In June of that year Taylor, who had become sufficiently alarmed by reports of Clare's increasingly desperate mental condition to seek professional help, recommended him to the private clinic of Dr Matthew Allen, at High Beach, Essex, on the edge of Epping Forest. Edward Storey tells us that a stranger arrived at the cottage with a message from Taylor, to the effect that 'Clare was to prepare himself for a journey: "the bearer will bring you up to town and take care of you on the way . . . the medical aid provided near to this place will cure you effectually" '. Clare wanted to stay and Patty pleaded on his behalf. But they were overridden. He had to go.

Taylor had chosen well. Commentators by and large agree that Allen was an enlightened and humane man. He did not believe in locking his patients up. They were encouraged to take part in healthy, outdoor exercise; and they were free to wander the extensive and attractive grounds of High Beach. Jane Carlyle thought Allen's asylum a place where any sane person would be delighted to be admitted. Given what she had to put up with at home this isn't perhaps quite the praise it may at first seem. But Tennyson also stayed there ('under what terms we no longer know', his biographer R. B. Martin says); and the great and the good seem to have been at one in their praise of Allen's institution.

But although Clare at first enjoyed Allen's company and the relaxed regimen of High Beach, he didn't recover. Of course he wrote poetry. There were many lyrics and ballads to and about Mary Joyce (who died in 1838), but none of them is among his best. Then there are *Child Harold* and *Don Juan*. The latter is full of good things. Clare was, as I have noted before, a marvellous mimic and he seems almost effortlessly to ape Byron's manner. But through the poem you can feel the ache of lost self-esteem and the desire to compensate for this in a dream of triumph: 'Though laurel wreathes my brows did ne'er environ/I think myself as great a bard as Byron'. Byron would have enjoyed the wit of that rhyme, but although Clare's poem is a *tour de force* what is most noticeable about it is his sense of *not* being Byron. He is in truth invisible.

Hence, the pathetic strategies by means of which he tried to make himself seen and heard. He drafted an advertisement for 'A New Vol of Poems by Lord Byron Not Yet Collected In His Works'; and he acquired, intermittently at least, a habit of heading each word with capitals. A letter to his wife begins: 'My Dear Patty It Makes Me More Than Happy To Hear That You & My Dear Family Are All Well'. And the first stanzas of the 'Song of Deborah' run:

In The War Days Of Shamgar Of Anath & Jael
When The High Ways Were Leveled & Hamlets Laid Low
& Every Heart Seemed In Its Courage To Fail
& Sought Out The Bye Ways In Fear Of The Foe

The Inhabitants Ceased In Each Village To Dwell
Desolation Drove Comfort From Mountain & Plain
Till I Even Deborah Rose To Foretell
That God Would Unite With His Chosen Again

It's as though this obsessive capitalization will make the words more visible, even empowered. And this is of a piece with Clare's assumption of the identity of the prize fighter Jack Randall, in whose name he issued 'A Challenge To All The World'.

But the 'Song of Deborah' is important for quite another reason.

Its detailed use of the Old Testament – in this case the Book of Judges – not only shows how deeply Clare's memory of the Bible was rooted within him, but why it should flower at this moment. His Deborah, prophetess, speaks of the oppression of village inhabitants, whose hamlets have been 'laid low', their inhabitants driven out by seemingly unopposable force. Clare is remembering *Judges* 5: 7, where the biblical Deborah says 'The inhabitants of the village ceased, they ceased in Israel, until that I Deborah arose, that I arose a mother in Israel'. As in 'The Lamentations of Round-Oak Waters' so here, Clare uses the Old Testament in a way common to nonconformity: as inspired text, the universal truths of which will apply to the personal circumstances of those latter-day children of Israel, the poor and afflicted of nineteenth-century England: their suffering has marked them out for God's special purpose, his promise to 'His Chosen'. There is a terrible poignancy about this. In the asylum at Essex, far away from family and from the fields of Helpston where enclosure has denied him the freedom to wander, Clare imagines himself into the voice of the rapt Jewish prophetess, inspiring her people to rise against their oppressors. And this rapture of distress breathes through what seems to me the best poetry of this first asylum period: his versions of 'Solomon's Prayer' and, especially, of Job chapters 38–41, that 'fine Hebrew poem' which had always exercised so deep a hold on his imagination.

By comparison, the natural scene mattered far less. It wasn't *his* and he was away from the language which gave it identity. In 1841, while still at High Beach, he drafted a letter to Mary Joyce, whose death he either didn't know about or refused to accept, in which he told her that 'nature to me seems dead & her very pulse seems frozen to an icicle in the summer sun'. And yet it may be that he *was* aware of her death. She had become indissolubly linked to the natural world. In one of the songs of *Child Harold*, Clare writes:

> How soft the dew falls on the leaves of the beeches
> How fresh the wild flower seems to slumber below
> How sweet are the lessons that nature still teaches
> For truth is her tidings wherever I go
> From schooldays of boyhood her image was cherished
> In manhood sweet Mary was fairer then flowers
> Nor yet has her name or her memory perished
> Though abscence like winter oer happiness lowers

Mary and the natural scene elide into one. Both are denied him. Allen, who understood much about Clare, never understood this most crucial matter. When he came to write about Clare's admission to the asylum, he noted that the poet was 'exceedingly miserable', that he bemoaned his poverty, and that 'given the excitement of excessive flattery at one time and neglect at another, his extreme poverty and over-exertion of body and mind' it was no wonder 'that his feeble frame, with his wonderful active powers of mind, was overcome'. All this is true, but it leaves out of account how for Clare loss of place was loss of love was, therefore, loss of self.

In the early summer of 1841 Clare wrote yet again to Mary, his 'first wife & first love'. 'No one knows how sick I am of this confinement', he told her. By July he had had enough. He made contact with some gipsies who were camped in woods near High Beach. They offered to hide him and help him escape, but on condition of payment, and Clare had no money. When he went back a few days later they had gone. All that remained of the campsite was an old hat. Clare put it into his pocket. Then he set out on the long walk home.

'The Riddle Nature Could Not Prove'

But there was no home. The last words of the harrowing prose account of his *Journey Out of Essex* are: 'July 24th 1841 Returned home out of Essex and found no Mary – her and her family are as nothing to me now though she herself was once dearest of all – and how can I forget'. *The Journey* recounts wandering and hardships, but it ends with no Odysseus-like triumph of recognition, no reconciliation between man and wife:

> a cart met me with a man and a boy in it when nearing me
> the woman jumped out and caught hold of my hands and wished
> me to get into the cart but I refused and thought her either
> drunk or mad but when told it was my second wife Patty I got
> in and was soon at Northborough but Mary was not there . . .
> so here I am homeless at home

He was not to stay there long. By Christmas 1841 Patty had become alarmed by his instability. As a result of her appeals, Dr Fenwick Skrimshire made application to have Clare admitted to Northampton General Asylum. Clare's madness, he said, had been brought on by 'years addicted to poetical prosings'. No blame attaches to Patty. Clare had turned violent and between bouts of terrible temper he would sit in a corner of their cottage muttering to himself. She was frightened both of and for him. When, on 29 December 1841, men arrived to take him away, she wept to see him struggle and at his cry to be left alone.

A number of visitors came to see him at the asylum. Among then was a Spencer T. Hall who in 1873 wrote up his interview with Clare as part of his *Biographical Sketches of Remarkable People*. According to Hall, at their meeting the poet told him he was in preparation for a prize fight and was proud of his fame as a fighter. Wasn't he prouder of his fame as a poet, Hall asked. 'Oh, poetry', Clare said. 'Ah, I know, I once had something to do with poetry, a long while ago; but it was no good.'

In fact he went on writing more or less until his death. Many of the late poems survive only in versions transcribed for him by the asylum's house-steward, W. F. Knight. As Robinson and Powell note in their Oxford edition, 'there is no guarantee of authenticity in the spelling, punctuation, grammar, or even vocabulary' of these poems, nor in ones set down by other amanuenses. On the other hand, punctuation and indentation apart, the following is hardly likely to have been much altered from Clare's intentions.

> Where hae ye been sae far awae
>   My fair creature?
> I've been by the mountain side
>   Whar the siller burnie glide
> I've been looking far, and wide
>   Farest creature

A goodly number of poems of the asylum years are written in a kind of Lallans, for all the world as though Clare is imagining himself into the skin of Burns, or James Hogg, 'the Ettrick Shepherd', or that other Scottish peasant poet, Robert Tannahill (1774–1810), whose songs we know that Clare greatly admired. He may have been drawn to imitate these poets because of their considerable fame (although it's just possible he identified with their unhappy lives: Burns died in poverty, Tannahill committed suicide and Hogg, though more fortunate than either, had to survive long years of hardship.) He certainly seems to have thought himself into the role of Scottish bard, rightly aware, no doubt, that in Scotland his kind of poet was more likely to be revered than scorned. One poem, 'Scotland', begins 'My heart is in Scotland, wi' nature sae grand,/Which seemed to me aince, my ain happy land:/When I gazed on the blue lake, and clomb the high brow;/It was my ain land then, and sae it seems now'. And this, though he'd never been further north than Stamford.

Some of the Scottish poems are addressed to Mary. So are many others written in an accent nearer his own. Although he knew she was dead he couldn't bring himself to accept the fact. He mourns her absence, as he calls it, 'the most severe', but he also says that 'she the soul of life for whom I sigh/Like flowers shall cheer me when the storm is bye'. That she *was* dead to him is, though, not so much evident in the poems which lament her 'abscence' as in ones which routinely praise nature. For here you do sense that Clare is bereft of the love which had charged much of his finest work. Mary/Nature/home (Helpston): the terms are interchangeable and interfused. All three were now lost to him and 'Mary' stands as the metonymy of that loss. 'To the Lark' begins: 'Bird of the morn/When roseate clouds begin/To shew the opening dawn/Thy singing does begin'; and it isn't merely the unnoticed repetition of 'begin' which suggests that here, as in many other late poems, Clare is simply going through the motions.

Just occasionally, though, something of the original freshness comes back. Here are the opening lines of 'The Round Oak'.

> The Apple Top't oak in the old narrow lane
> And the hedgerow of bramble and thorn
> Will ne'er throw their green on my visions again
> As they did on that sweet dewy morn
> When I went for spring pooteys and birds nest to look
> Down the border of bushes ayont the fair spring
> I gathered the palm grass close to the brook
> And heard the sweet birds in thorn bushes sing

But this effort to recall lea close oak, which had been cut down as part of the act of enclosure (and which Clare had written about in 'Remembrances'), itself explains why the poem, and others like it, can't sustain for long the loving, exact description of his earlier work. More than any other poet I can think of, Clare depended on being able to see and hear that 'real world' where he delighted to wander, which he knew with an intense, intimate regard, and where what was known could be named. That he could still recover that vision, for a brief while at least, is clear from a handful of poems, of which the magic, inimitable 'Little Trotty Wagtail' is an outstanding example; but for the most part, as he said, the 'scenes' he had known couldn't 'throw their green on my visions again'. Their active presence was doubly denied him as it had been at High Beach: by enclosure and by his removal from his 'native scene'.

As a result, the finest poems of the asylum years tend to be those in which, astoundingly enough, he manages to write with absolute lucidity about the dissolution of his sense of selfhood. There is, for

example, the sonnet which begins 'Enough of misery keeps my heart
alive/To make it feel more mental agony' – although towards the
end it does I think become confused; there is 'Written in Prison', and
there are others. Without doubt the greatest of them is the three-
stanza poem called 'I Am'.

1

I am – yet what I am, none cares or knows;
   My friends forsake me like a memory lost: –
I am the self-consumer of my woes; –
   They rise and vanish in oblivion's host,
Like shadows in love's frenzied stifled throes:
   And yet I am, and live – like vapours tost

2

Into the nothingness of scorn and noise, –
   Into the living sea of waking dreams,
Where there is neither sense of life or joys,
   But the vast shipwreck of my lifes esteems;
Even the dearest, that I love the best
   Are strange – nay, rather stranger than the rest.

3

I long for scenes, where man hath never trod
   A place where woman never smiled or wept
There to abide with my Creator, God;
   And sleep as I in childhood, sweetly slept,
Untroubling, and untroubled where I lie,
   The grass below – above the vaulted sky.

Clare can't possibly have wanted the poem to look like this, with its
heavy punctuation and ludicrous numbering of stanzas (apart from
anything else, this entirely wrecks the move across from the first to
second stanza). Like Cowper's 'Lines Written During a Period of
Insanity', and Hopkins's 'terrible' sonnets, Clare's poem is written
in extremis and yet manages to be about his condition in a manner
that defies any reader to think of it as anything other than a true
poem. Nor does it slide into self-pity. He isn't wishing himself into
his grave. Instead, he yearns with hopeless intensity for a pre-
lapsarian, unfallen, unenclosed world, free from both the allure and
sufferings of women and the threatening tread of men.

And yet at about the same time he wrote that letter he also wrote
this a 'song' although it often goes under the title of 'Song' ballad

To John Clare

Well honest John how fare you now at home
The spring is come and birds are building nests
The old cock robin to the sty is come
With olive feathers and its ruddy breast
And the old cock with red combs and red comb
Struts with the hens and seems to like some bell
Then crows and looks about for little crumbs

Select Bibliography

BIBLIOGRAPHIES

As far as I know there is as yet no comprehensive bibliography of the writings of John Clare. There is however a helpful *Descriptive Catalogue of the John Clare Collection* in Peterborough Museum and Art Gallery, prepared for the museum by Margaret Grainger and published in 1973.

EDITIONS OF WORKS BY JOHN CLARE

Poetry

Collections
The two-volume collected *Poems of John Clare*, ed. J. W. Tibble (London: Dent, 1935) is now in the process of being superseded by the vastly expensive edition prepared by Eric Robinson and David Powell and published by OUP. Unfortunately even this edition fails to include a number of pencil sketches which Clare made to accompany particular poems, and which he clearly thought of as integral to them.

Selections and collections of individual volumes
There are various editions of single volumes of Clare's work. They include:

The Midsummer Cushion, ed. Anne Tibble (Manchester: Carcanet/MidNAG, 1978).
The Parish, ed. Eric Robinson (Harmondsworth: Viking/Penguin, 1983). This contains a helpful introduction and notes.
The Rural Muse, ed. R. K. R. Thornton (Manchester: Carcanet/MidNAG, 1982).
The Shepherd's Calendar, eds. Eric Robinson and Geoffrey Summerfield (Oxford: OUP, 1964; since reprinted). The introduction is good on Taylor's editorial interference with the first edition of 1827.

There are various selections of Clare's poetry (and, sometimes, prose) to choose from. Among the best are:

John Clare: The Oxford Author Series, eds. Eric Robinson and David Powell (Oxford, 1984). This generous selection of Clare's poetry and prose is undoubtedly the most accurate there is and is supported by helpful annotation as well as a glossary of Northamptonshire words. The selection is marred, however, by the editors' decision to bring together many of Clare's bird poems, regardless of chronology. This blurs distinctions between the very different moments and contexts which prompted Clare to compose them.

John Clare: Selected Poems, eds. J. W. and Anne Tibble (London: Dent/ Everyman, 1965). A wide-ranging selection. The texts are inferior but the glossary is full.

John Clare: Selected Poetry, ed. Geoffrey Summerfield (Harmondsworth: Penguin, 1990). Summerfield groups the poems according to subject rather than chronology, but his love and intimate knowledge of Clare's work, together with his notes, make this idiosyncratic selection well worth having.

John Clare: Selected Poetry and Prose, eds. Merryn and Raymond Williams (London: Methuen, 1986). The introduction is good, as is the choice and accuracy of the texts. The annotation and critical commentary are, however, poor and sometimes misleading.

Prose

The Natural History Prose Writings of John Clare, ed. Margaret Grainger (OUP, 1983). A splendidly full and impeccably edited edition.

John Clare's Autobiographical Writings, ed. Eric Robinson (Oxford: OUP 1983). Important because Robinson prints the best text we have of *Sketches in the Life of John Clare Written by Himself*. There is also helpful annotation.

The Prose of John Clare, eds. J. W. and Anne Tibble (London: Routledge & Kegan Paul, 1951). The text is less reliable than Robinson's but there is more of it, together with interesting illustrations and notes.

John Clare: The Journals, Essays, and Journey Out of Essex, ed. Anne Tibble (Manchester: Carcanet, 1980).

Letters

The Letters of John Clare, ed. Mark Storey (Oxford: OUP, 1985). This fully annotated edition is now the standard edition of the letters.

John Clare: Selected Letters, ed. Mark Storey (Oxford: OUP, 1988). A helpful selection from Storey's impeccable edition of 1985.

BIOGRAPHICAL AND CRITICAL STUDIES

Barrell, John, *The Idea of Landscape and the Sense of Place, 1730–1840: An Approach to the Poetry of John Clare* (Cambridge: CUP, 1972). A work of inestimable importance.

—*The Dark Side of Landscape* (Cambridge: CUP, 1980).

—'John Clare, William Cobbett and the Changing Landscape', in *From Blake to Byron*, New Pelican Guide to English Literature, ed. Boris Ford (Harmondsworth: Penguin, 1982).

Brownlow, T., *John Clare and the Picturesque Landscape* (Oxford: OUP, 1983).

Chilcott, T., *A Real World and a Doubting Mind: A Critical Study of the Poetry of John Clare* (Pickering: Hull University Press, 1985).

Clare, Johanne, *John Clare and the Bounds of Circumstance* (Kingston and Montreal: McGill-Queen's University Press, 1987). One of the best critical studies.

Crossan, G., *A Relish for Eternity: The Process of Divinization in the Poetry of John Clare*, Salzburg Studies in English Literature, 53, 1976.

Deacon, George, *John Clare and the Folk Tradition* (Sinclair and Browne, 1983). This uniquely important study surveys the tradition of folk song and ballad which Clare loved and which prompted and fed into much of his work. Deacon transcribes the tunes of ballads which Clare himself transcribed, most if not all of which he learned to 'scrat' on his violin.

Frosch, T. R., 'The Descriptive Style of John Clare', *Studies in Romanticism*, 10, Spring 1971.

Grigson, G., *Poems of John Clare's Madness* (London: Routledge & Kegan Paul, 1949). Although Grigson's text is not to be trusted, his long introduction is well worth reading.

Haughton, H., and Phillips, A. (eds.), *John Clare in Context*. This is the provisional title for a collection of critical essays, to be published by Cambridge University Press in 1994.

Howkins, A., and I. C. Dyck, ' "The Time's Alterations": Popular Ballads, Rural Radicals and William Cobbett', *History Workshop*, 23, Spring 1987.

Jack, I., 'Poems of John Clare's Sanity', in J. Logan, J. Jordan, N. Frye (eds.), *Some British Romantics* (Columbus: Ohio State University Press, 1966).

John Clare Society Journal. Appears annually and regularly contains essays of interest.

Keith, W. J., *The Poetry of Nature: Rural Perspectives in Poetry from Wordsworth to the Present* (Toronto: University of Toronto Press, 1980).

Lucas, John, *England and Englishness: Ideas of Nationhood in English Poetry, 1688–1900* (London: Chatto & Windus, 1990; pb. edn. 1991). Includes a chapter on Clare.

—'England in 1830: Wordsworth, Clare, and the question of poetic authority', in *Critical Survey*, vol. 2, no. 1, 1992.

—'Places and dwellings: Wordsworth, Clare and the anti-picturesque', in D. Cosgrove and S. Daniels (eds.), *The Iconography of Landscape* (Cambridge: CUP, 1988; pb. edn. 1989).

—'Revising Clare', in R. Brinkley and K. Hanley (eds.), *Romantic Revisions* (Cambridge: CUP, 1992).

Martin, F., *The Life of John Clare* (1865; London: Frank Cass, 1964). The republished text of this lively, sympathetic biography has an introduction and notes by Robinson and Summerfield.

Minor, M., 'John Clare and the Methodists: A Reconsideration', *Studies in Romanticism*, 19, Spring 1980.

Paulin, T., 'John Clare in Babylon', in T. Paulin, *Minotaur: Poetry and the Nation State* (London: Faber, 1992).

Storey, E., *A Right to Song: The Life of John Clare* (London: Methuen, 1982).

Storey, M., *The Poetry of John Clare: A Critical Introduction* (London: Macmillan, 1974).

—(ed.), *Clare: The Critical Heritage* (London: Routledge & Kegan Paul, 1973). An indispensable work, containing contemporary reviews and comments on Clare's work. Storey's notes are full and helpful.

Strang, Barbara, 'John Clare's Language', in R. K. R. Thornton (ed.), *The Rural Muse*, (Manchester: Carcanet/MidNAG, 1982).

Swingle, L. J., 'Stalking the Essential John Clare: Clare in Relation to his Romantic Contemporaries', *Studies in Romanticism*, 14, Summer 1975.

Tibble, Anne, *John Clare: A Life* (London: Michael Joseph, 1972). This is a revised version of the biography by both Tibbles, first published in 1932.

Todd, Janet, *In Adam's Garden: A Study of John Clare's Pre-Asylum Poetry* (Gainsville: University of Florida Press, 1973).

Wade, Stephen, 'John Clare's Use of Dialect', in *Contemporary Review*, 223, August 1973.

Wilson, June, *Green Shadows: The Life of John Clare* (London: Hodder & Stoughton, 1951).

OTHER RELEVANT WORKS

Abbott, C. C., *The Life and Letters of George Darley, Poet and Critic* (Oxford: Clarendon Press, 1928; repr. 1967). Useful on literary life in London during the 1820s. Darley was for a while a friend of Clare's.

Browne, Ford K., *Fathers of the Victorians* (Cambridge: CUP, 1961). Important because of its study of evangelicalism and of Radstock's place within the movement.

Chilcott, T., *A Publisher and his Circle: The Life and Works of John Taylor, Keats's Publisher* (London: Routledge & Kegan Paul, 1972). Given that Taylor was also Clare's publisher, Chilcott's monograph has much to say that is of interest to the student of Clare.

Cobbett, W., *Cottage Economy* (1821–2; Oxford Paperback, 1979).

—*Rural Rides* (1830). Republished with an introduction and notes by George Woodcock (Harmondsworth: Penguin, 1967).

Corrigan, P., and Sayer, D., *The Great Arch: English State Formation as Cultural Revolution* (Oxford: Basil Blackwell, 1985).

Davies, P., *Methodism* (Harmondsworth: Penguin, 1972).

Elliott, Ebenezer, *The Poetical Works* (Edinburgh: William Tait, 1840). There is no modern edition of poems of the 'Corn-Law Rhymer', and the two-volume edition edited by Elliott's son drops many of the important notes which the Tait edition retains.

Green, D., *Great Cobbett: The Noblest Agitator* (Oxford: OUP, 1985). The fullest and most informative of available biographies.

Halévy, E., *A History of the English People in the Nineteenth Century*, vol. 1, *The Liberal Awakening* (1926; London: Benn, 1961). Halévy is in many respects superseded, but his account of the rise of radical newspapers in the later years of the 1820s is still essential reading.

Hammond, J. L. and Barbara, *The Village Labourer 1760–1832* (London: Longmans, Green, 1911). A classic study which, despite attacks on it from those historians who have chosen to concentrate on the benefits of enclosure and improved agricultural methods during the period covered by the Hammonds' study, nevertheless survives virtually unscathed as an unforgettable account of what enclosure meant to those who had to suffer it.

Harker, D., *Fakesong: The Manufacture of British 'folksong' 1700 to the present day* (Milton Keynes: Open University Press, 1967). Among much else, Harker criticizes those like A. L. Lloyd (see below) who have tried to argue for a line of folk song surviving in 'pure' form. The evidence he produces helps to show the kinds of process of adaptation with which Clare was familiar.

Henderson, H., *Alias MacAlias* (Edinburgh: Polygon, 1993). Henderson's numerous essays on folk song are gathered here, and between them restate the 'classic' position about the transmission of songs. But Henderson also shows how, in the Scottish tradition at least, 'high' and 'low' ballads could interpretate in a manner that Wordsworth hoped to achieve in his Lyrical Ballads, and that Clare, whom Henderson does not mention, succeeded in doing.

Hobsbawm, E., and Rudé, G., *Captain Swing* (London: Lawrence & Wishart, 1969; pb. edn. Pimlico, 1993). The definitive study of the agricultural riots that affected most of southern England and the midland counties in the last years of the 1820s.

Lloyd, A. L., *Folk Song in England* (London: Lawrence & Wishart, 1967; pb. edn. Paladin, 1975). Despite Harker's substantial criticisms this book remains useful because, whatever the demerits of its scholarship and the theoretical position on which Lloyd's arguments are based, his compendious knowledge of folk song and ballad makes him a necessary reference point for anyone interested in studying Clare.

Lucas, John, *From Romantic to Modern Literature: Essays and Ideas of Culture, 1750–1900* (Sussex: Harvester Press, 1982). See the essays on 'The Idea of the Provincial' (for discussion of the changing meanings of the words 'vulgar' and 'common' between 1750 and 1830) and 'Wordsworth and the anti-Picturesque', for an account of the politics of the picturesque.

Martin, G. B., *Tennyson: The Unquiet Heart* (Oxford: Clarendon and Faber, 1980). Of interest because Martin provides a chapter on Dr Matthew Allen and his private sanitorium, High Beach, where Clare stayed from 1837 to 1841.

Neeson, J., 'The Disappearance of the English Peasantry, Revisited', in *Agricultural Organization in the Century of Industrialization: Europe, Russia and North America in the 19th Century, Research in Economic History*, Supplement 5, 1989.

—'The Opponents of Enclosure in 18th century Northamptonshire', *Past and Present*, 105, 1984.

These two fine essays by Neeson have much to say of relevance to Clare and his mingled anger and despair at what was being done to him and his neighbourhood as enclosure took hold. To be read alongside the Hammonds' work.

Newby, H., *The Deferential Worker* (Allen & Unwin, 1977). Newby develops Gramsci's argument that agricultural labourers develop a contradictory 'tactic' of being at one and the same time rebellious against and deferential to authority.

Reay, B., *The Last Rising of the Agricultural Worker* (Oxford: OUP, 1990).

Reid, J. C., *Thomas Hood* (London: Routledge & Kegan Paul, 1963). Hood knew Clare and, like him though more successfully, struggled to make a living by writing for the market, especially in the verses he supplied for journals and magazines, to many of which Clare also contributed.

Thomas, K., *Man and the Natural World* (London: Allen Lane, 1983). Interesting on the growth of the study of natural history in the late eighteenth and nineteenth centuries.

Thompson, E. P., *The Making of the English Working Class* (London: Gollancz, 1963; Harmondsworth: Pelican, 1967).

—*Customs in Common* (London: Merlin Press, 1991). No one wishing to understand Clare can afford to ignore these two great books by Thompson.

Unwin, R., *The Rural Muse: Studies in the Peasant Poetry of England* (London: George Allen and Unwin, 1954). Useful in that Unwin mentions enough names to give some sense of the tradition into which Clare could be slotted by those anxious to market him as a 'peasant poet'.

Vincent, D., *Bread, Knowledge and Freedom: A Study of the 19th century working-class autobiography* (London: Methuen, 1981). Has the effect of showing how early Clare's venture into autobiography was, and also provides a useful context in which to consider why Clare should want to write a prose account of his own life.

—'The Decline of the Oral Tradition in Popular Culture', in R. Storch (ed.), *Popular Culture and Custom in Nineteenth Century England* (London: Croom Helm, 1982). The title of this excellent essay explains its relevance to Clare.

Wickett, W., and Duval, N., *The Farmer's Boy: The Story of a Suffolk Poet, Robert Bloomfield, His Life and Poems, 1766–1823*. This offers a sketch of Bloomfield's life and prints a small selection of his poems, including 'My Old Oak Table', on which Clare drew for his great poem, 'To A Fallen Elm'. There is no biography of Bloomfield and no modern edition of his poems. We badly need both, but until they are forthcoming Wickett and Duval's book, limited as it is, remains the best we have.

Williams, R., *The Country and the City* (pb. London: Paladin, 1975). Important for Williams's de-mystifying of the images of rural England as a place of contentment and 'rooted' values.

Worrall, D., *Radical Culture: Discourse, Resistance and Surveillance, 1790–1820* (Hemel Hempstead: Harvester/Wheatsheaf, 1992). Worrall valuably focuses on showing how radicals in this period were motivated by a campaign to return the land to the people. Although Worrall does not discuss Clare, his book makes plain that the language of radical protest developed by the groups he does study feeds into much of Clare's poetry.

Index

85